MODERN
AMERICAN
HISTORY ★ A

Garland
Series

Edited by
FRANK FREIDEL
Harvard University

A HISTORY OF
THE ECONOMIC ANALYSIS
OF THE GREAT DEPRESSION
IN AMERICA

William E. Stoneman

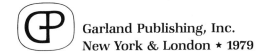

Garland Publishing, Inc.
New York & London ★ 1979

Library of Congress Cataloging in Publication Data

Stoneman, William E., 1939–
  A history of the economic analysis of the great
depression in America.

  (Modern American history)
  Originally presented as the author's thesis, Harvard
University, 1969.
  Bibliography: p.
  1. Depressions—1929—United States. 2. United
States—Economic conditions—1918–1945.
3. Economics—United States—History. I. Title.
II. Series.
HB3717.1929.S75   1979   338.5'4'0973   78-62514
ISBN 0-8240-3640-9

All volumes in this series are printed on acid-free,
250-year-life paper.
Printed in the United States of America

A HISTORY OF THE ECONOMIC ANALYSIS
OF THE GREAT DEPRESSION
IN AMERICA

<u>Preface</u>, August 1978

It was not until the 1970's that Inflation
definitively usurped the place of Depression as our
economic nightmare. True, popular culture betrays
a certain uneasiness that our current inflation may
someday lead again into Depression. But for nearly
all economists the practical task at hand is to check
the tendency toward inflation.

Still it may be well to preface this dissertation,
written in 1969, with just a word of caution for the
general reader who may be expecting "history to repeat
itself", and our prosperity once more to succumb to
Great Depression. To hobble at the outset possible
abuses of analogy, let it be mentioned that the 1920's
<u>were</u> <u>not</u> <u>an</u> <u>inflationary</u> <u>period</u>, and indeed saw ever
so slightly falling prices from the midpoint of the
decade onward. At the time this was taken (believe
it or not) to indicate a great stability, and a relative
absence of speculative excess, overbuilding, and
general frothiness. Later analysts have had to see

in the price weakness of the 1920's one of the (few) warning signals that potential Depression lay ahead.

If another Depression is in store for us, it ought to be fairly clear by now that it will evolve largely through policies employed in the battle against inflation. The sharp contraction of 1974-75 came about partly or perhaps mainly in that fashion. The Federal Reserve choked off the growth in money supply, bringing down economic activity along with price inflation. Thus we have entered a period in which business cycles are more and more entirely "policy cycles", often referred to as "stop-and-go" policy cycles.

These have very little in common with the business cycles of our history prior to 1933. Therefore, it is not for analogy but for contrast that one would need to study the Great Depression. During the 1920's government spending (at local, state, and federal levels) comprised roughly 10% of gross national product. Since World War II it has mainly hovered around 30%, where it remains today. Most economists would probably agree--though some grudgingly, and others not at all--that these high and rather predictably rising levels of government spending are what have kept us from Depression since the War. By this token, one might fairly speculate that the most likely cause of another Depression would be a "tax-revolt" that actually succeeded in paring government spending to 10-20% of GNP. That might be a policy cycle literally to end them all, and restore us to the boom-bust economy that held sway in 1921-33. And the dominant products of the private economy today are not very different from those of the 1920's.

Needless to say, such a revolution in government policy is far from likely. And today, with the federal government running a $50 billion annual deficit, those who propose government spending cuts as an antidote to inflation are on very strong ground, and may not be accused of seeking to plunge us back into the morass of the thirties. All in all, it is a sound generalization that the reaction against the Depression of the 1930's, and the laborious construction of governmental supports to economic activity from 1933 through the 1960's--that this reaction was indeed the cause of today's inflation. In particular the years after 1965 saw governmental overstimulation, both fiscal and monetary, which is generally agreed to have launched a chronic tendency toward inflation, and even a credible menace of Great Inflation.

So perhaps it should not be surprising that misinformation about the Great Depression, and ignorance of its economic

literature, are now more widespread--even among economists--
than ever before. This is undoubtedly due mainly to lack of
serious interest. Economists are busy searching for ways of
attacking inflation, and its bizarre stepchild "inflation-
recession". On the rare occasions when economists refer to
the Depression, it is usually in a more or less off-hand way,
and comes in the midst of an earnest commentary on today's
inflation. Analogies are often strained; for as we urged
above, there simply are not many good analogies to be made.

And yet, over the last ten years, a kind of consensus-
by-default has been forming about the Depression. It evolved
out of monetarist economics, and as monetarism gradually has
come to predominance in economics, so has this interpretation
of the Depression gained acceptance. In approaching any
economic problem, monetarists give primary emphasis to trends
in the overall supply of money in the economy and banking
system. Monetarism is neither new in the history of economic
analysis, nor is it in a theoretical sense "opposed" to the
Keynesian economics that came to maturity during and after
the Depression. A Keynesian economist pays attention to
monetary policy along with fiscal policy. A monetarist is
unlikely to ignore fiscal policy. Monetarism has sometimes
seemed opposed to Keynesian economics, because many monetarists

favor a reduction in government spending and regulation. But
this they favor for its own sake, and not because such an
advocacy is intrinsic to the study of monetary affairs or the
practice of monetary policy.

Yet when it comes to the analysis of the Depression, monetarism has taken on a perhaps more distinct meaning. This
may have occurred almost by accident, when the man who was to
become the leading monetarist economist, Milton Friedman,
espoused a certain view of the Depression. Friedman, together
with Anna Schwartz, wrote A Monetary History of the United
States, 1867-1960.[1] The book, published in 1963, was a magnifi-
cently detailed effort, and went far to define monetarism as
a developed field of economics. Its good-sized chapter on
the Depression seems similarly to have determined the future
course of monetarist interpretation of the Depression, even
though it need not have. For the major purpose of the chapter
was to set forth in depth how the Federal Reserve System could
have, but did not, fight off the Depression in 1930-32.

Friedman and Schwartz argue that the Federal Reserve

---

[1]. The book was published for the National Bureau of Economic Research, by Princeton University Press.
In these footnotes, we will refer to the free-standing paperback
edition of the chapter on the Depression, The Great Contraction
1929-1933 (Princeton, 1965), since it contains a Preface which
expresses the authors' views even more unqualifiedly than the
original volume did.

ought to have undertaken massive open-market purchases of U.S.
government bonds from the banks. This would have increased
the liquidity and solvency of the banks, encouraged lending
to business, and perhaps reversed the tide of Depression and
bankruptcy.[2] It is a grand essay in policy that might-have-
been, and few would deny that the policy might have worked.
Yet qua interpretation of the severity of the Depression, the
Friedman-Schwartz thesis is not well developed. It amounts
to a few opening remarks to the effect that a contraction in
the money supply was a chief cause of the Depression.[3]

In preparing this dissertation in 1969, this writer
considered the Friedman-Schwartz interpretation a very minor
contribution to the lengthy literature of the Depression, and
relegated it to a small footnote. Since it has proved quite
durable, it obviously must be discussed further now. The
interpretation has a strained quality which is revealed by
the handsome charts and graphs appended for reference by the
authors. The charts show a very small decline in the money
supply (the authors compute it at 2.6%) during the first year
of the Depression from late 1929 to late 1930. Yet in the
same period of time, industrial production fell roughly 20%,

[2.] Great Contraction, Preface, pp. 4-5, 15, 17-18, and passim.

[3.] Ibid., pp. 3-4, 11-12 .

wholesale prices roughly 10%, consumer prices 4%.[4] The
initial thrust of the Depression, one would tend to conclude,
came from industrial production rather than money supply.
Thinking further, one must add as well that since prices fell
faster than money supply, the supply of money in real terms
actually rose in the first year of Depression!

This is not a complicated point. Just as we have learned
to correct for inflation in calculating the real value of
money today, we must correct for price deflation during the
Depression. Whether real or nominal money supply is the more
useful quantity for economic forecasting and policy-making,
happens recently to have become a burning issue among economists. It is a fascinating issue, and for various reasons
may be very difficult to resolve. But a study of purely
historical data that does not point out a flat contradiction
between the trends of nominal money supply and real money
supply, can no longer be considered a finished study. And
while some economists might still maintain that the fall in
nominal money supply 1929-30 was at least a modest depressant,
others might argue that the rise in real money should have
provided a major support for the economy.

[4.] Ibid. pp. 2, 5, 11. The consumer price fall is derived
from the statistics on p.5.

viii

From late 1930 onward, Friedman and Schwartz date a
series of progressively more serious "banking crises", culminating in the national banking holidays of early 1933. By that
time over one fifth of the commercial banks in the nation
(which had held nearly one tenth of the volume of deposits as
of 1929) had already suspended operations.[5] This trend, of
course, exerted downward pressure on the supply of money and
on economic activity overall.

But again referring to the Friedman-Schwartz charts (and
they have never been seriously questioned as statistical guide-
lines), one must note that industrial production continued
year after year to fall faster than money supply. By mid-1932
industrial production had fallen over 50% from the 1929 peak,
and as a matter of fact began to recover. Even the final banking crisis and holidays failed to drive industrial production
back to its lows of 1932; and a sharp recovery was again under
way by mid-1933.[6] This was probably based on hopes that
Roosevelt's New Deal would turn the tide; and also on renewed
inventory building after three years of collapse. Since unemployment never went above roughly 25% of the labor force, in
a general sense it may be said that the 50% drop in industrial

---

[5.] *Ibid.*, p.3.

[6.] *Ibid.*, p.2.

production had to be self-correcting at some point, and at
least to some extent.

But money supply fell, during the four years of the
Depression from 1929 to 1933, by smaller amounts: 2%, 7%, 17%
and 12%.[7] The worst decline occurred 1931-32, just as industrial production made ready for its recovery. And this
recovery progressed even in the face of the further 12% drop
in money supply in 1932-33. All in all, a very strong _prima_
facie case can be made that in the Collapse industrial production was a "leading indicator", money supply a "lagging" one,
which mainly registered after a time-lag the declines in production, employment, and payrolls.[8] Again, this is not to deny
that a concerted effort by the Federal Reserve to expand the
money supply might have checked the course of the Depression.
But that is a far different issue from whether money supply
was a major "cause" of the Collapse.

Another frailty in the argument of Friedman and Schwartz

7. _Ibid._, pp. 5-6. The first year's drop is 2% instead of
the 2.6% mentioned earlier, because the authors changed to a
different method of calculation, one based on annual averages.

8. Though it did not fall as fast as industrial production,
"real income" also fell faster than money supply, up until 1932-
33. It dropped in the four years 1929-33 by these amounts: 11%,
9%, 18%, and 3%. As for "real money supply", it _rose_ in 1930-
31 just as in 1929-30, and did not begin to fall until 1931-32.
From the Friedman-Schwartz statistics, one may compute that
consumer prices fell in the four years by 4%, 11%, 9%, and 2%.
(Wholesale prices fell still faster). Cf. _Ibid._, p. 5.

gradually makes itself felt. Much of the argument concerns
the irresolute or tardy action of the Federal Reserve System;
but the charts showing what in fact was done are not entirely
consonant with the textual descriptions of what was done. The
charts show that the Federal Reserve quickly brought down the
"discount rate" (the interest rate at which banks can borrow
from the Federal Reserve). At the time of the stock market
crash in the autumn of 1929, the discount rate was at 6% (having
been raised from 5% precisely to discourage further speculation
in stocks). It was brought down to 4½% by the end of 1929,
then by stages down to 2% by the end of 1930, and even to 1½%
in mid-1931.[9] This was forthright action to encourage bank
borrowing and extension of credit. And Friedman and Schwartz
do not discuss it seriously enough.

Interest rates measure the supply and demand for money.
Commercial paper rates (rates on certain kinds of loans to
businesses) are one of the better measurements of business
demand for money. And commercial paper rates moved downward
nearly as fast as the discount rate in the early Depression:
from 6% in late 1929 to just under 2% in mid-1931.[10] On the
face of it, one would have to say that business was not a

---

[9] Ibid., p. 8.
[10] Ibid., p.8.

highly active bidder for money. The implication is that the demand for money was what lacked, rather than the supply. And the bankers who opposed Federal Reserve action to inflate the money supply at the time--as quoted by Friedman and Schwartz-- were making just this point: if business will not borrow, invest, and expand, what good will creating more money do?[11]

So the last word on what the Federal Reserve could have done to combat the Depression has not been spoken. Nor can it ever be, since not history but historical speculation is at issue. We have gone into this discussion only because growing numbers of economists seem to feel that Friedman and Schwartz did speak the last word in 1963. Perhaps the best evidence of this faith is an article which appeared in the January 1975 issue of the influential journal Foreign Affairs.[12] Its title was "A World Depression?", and its argument that the recession of 1974-75 was not likely to proceed very far. Its authors, (monetarist) economists H. Cleveland and W. Brittain, make the general point that government agencies today are too committed to keeping up employment ever to allow a recession to become Depression. Then they go on to an extended discussion of the Great Depression as well as recent inflation.

[11] Ibid., pp. 75-77.

[12] H. Cleveland and W. Brittain, "A World Depression?", Foreign Affairs, v. 53, January 1975, pp. 223-241.

The article as a whole is an excellent and concise one.
However the analysis of the Depression runs on with complete
disregard for the painstaking economic debate over the Depression which stretched, quite unresolved, over the previous four
decades. The authors flatly state that contraction of the
money supply "caused"the Great Depression, as though the few
words of Friedman and Schwartz in 1963 had now become the
solidest of orthodoxies.[13] Not even the stock market crash of
1929 is mentioned as a partial cause of the Depression, though
economists concerned with monetary and financial factors have
traditionally given it weight. (Friedman and Schwartz too had
given it a role as an aggravating factor, though without dwelling
heavily on the point.)

The Cleveland-Brittain charts undermine their text just as
the Friedman-Schwartz charts do. A miniscule decline in money
supply in 1929 is shown for America. And another chart, picturing
the combined money supply of the United States, Britain, Germany,
and France, shows a slight _increase_ for 1929, and but a minor
decline in 1930.[14] As for the problem of real money supply,
no mention of it is made outside the authors' discussion of
the present-day situation (where it appears only fitfully).

---

13. Ibid., p. 223.
14. Ibid.,,p. 230.

Yet in their treatment of recent inflation, the authors'
argument is most convincing. They assert that the inflationary
burst of 1973-74 was caused by an increase in the rate of
growth of money supply in the largest industrial countries.
The rate rose from a previous average of 7% per annum to 12%
for the two years 1971-72; price inflation quickly got out
of hand in 1973-74. The authors' charts provide vivid testi-
mony, with the explosion in money supply clearly presaging
the upsurge in prices.[15]

Few economists would deny that when overall economic
activity is brisk, a rapid expansion of the money supply will
lead to price inflation. As will be seen in the study to
follow, economically buoyant periods normally see a rise in
the influence of monetarism upon economists. This occurred
in the mid-1920's, when some economists argued that the
business cycle could be overcome by monetary stimulation.
And again after 1950, as the basic strength of the economy
was established, interest in the possibilities of monetary
policy steadily advanced. Perhaps inevitably, monetary
stimulus was overdone by 1971-72; inflation replaced recession
as the dominant worry of economists; and monetarism became
the dominant mode of economic analysis.

And so it may remain. After all, monetary policy is

[15.] _Ibid._, pp. 233-237.

mainly controlled by the independent Federal Reserve, while
fiscal policy must be agreed upon by Congress and the President.
And as long as spending tends to run to inflationary deficits,
a close watch will necessarily be kept on monetary policy.
Unfortunately, when the latter was used against inflation in
1974, it produced a severe recession without finally ending
inflation. Evidently the wage-price spiral has already become
so entrenched as to defy both monetary and fiscal policy, or
any combination of them that has been tried.

As a sense of honest frustration spreads through the
economic community, perhaps the extreme fascination with monetary policy will abate. In any event, for the study of the
Depression it has done damage enough. In essence, the concerns
of an inflationary economy in which stop-and-go (monetary)
policy cycles hold sway, gradually suffused the profession's
thinking about the Great Depression. But that catastrophe
evolved in the course of a free-wheeling business cycle over
which government had little control, and sought little control.
And so to approach it we must rid ourselves of the preoccupations of contemporary economics.

Moreover, since in recent years economists have had so
little to say about the Depression, we have no choice but to
concentrate our reading in the years when it was the intel-

lectual challenge of the era. The largest part of the analysis treated in the following study was written in the 1930's. And while we can find no ultimate agreement among analysts, we can make out some intriguing patterns which tend towards agreement at several junctures between 1933 and the 1960's. In any case, we do learn much in reviewing one of the grand efforts in the history of thought.

William E. Stoneman
New York City

A HISTORY OF THE ECONOMIC ANALYSIS OF

THE GREAT DEPRESSION IN AMERICA

A thesis presented

by

William E. Stoneman

to

The History Department

in partial fulfillment of the requirements

for the degree of

Doctor of Philosophy

in the subject of

History

Harvard University

Cambridge, Massachusetts

June 1969

TABLE OF CONTENTS

INTRODUCTION

There is little doubt that America led the international economic recovery of the 1920's, and then overwhelmed it in the Collapse of the thirties. This dissertation is an account of the evolving analytical effort to comprehend the economic transition which took place in America during that interwar period. Since America had become the most influential economic power in the world, it should be no surprise that she possessed most of the economists who developed the interpretation of her economic experience. It will be necessary to deal with a number of economists--including important foreign ones-- but fortunately a handful of men will adequately embody the major interpretative trends from the later 1920's onward. There will not be space for rounded biographies of these figures, and focus will be drawn to the creative apices of their careers. Inevitably most important will be Wesley Mitchell as of the late 1920's, John Maurice Clark in the early thirties, Joseph Schumpeter in the 1930's, and Alvin Hansen from 1930 into the 1950's. The work of Hansen and Schumpeter might be expected to provide a center of gravity for this study. On the contrary, the

-1-

contribution of J. M. Clark of Columbia will occupy the
most pivotal place here. This will serve both to clarify
interpretative transitions, and to document, for its own
interest, Clark's unique and peculiarly American approach
to economics.

This emphasis will not be all-absorbing, but will
in the end clearly represent the argumentative germ of
this thesis. Keynes, by the same token, while integral to
analytic developments from 1930 to 1936 (<u>The General
Theory</u>)--will not emerge as a truly dominant figure.
Though his contribution was indeed a general and theoretical milestone of the era, it was in no sense definitive
for the interpretative conundra of the American breakdown.
On these matters there was an important tension between
Keynes and Hansen, and a still more productive debate
between Hansen, Schumpeter, and others. These debaters,
in turn, will be treated with attention to the prior work
of Clark, culminated in 1934, which had only partly been
incorporated into their ideas. Simply put, Clark's work
embodied the most dynamic approach to economic history:
i.e., it was oriented to great and irresistably unfolding
cycles of prosperity and depression. The Keynesian idea,
and for the most part the American construction of it by
Hansen, were designed to explain a whole era of generally
depressed activity--a natural preoccupation for the middle
and late thirties.

As will finally be suggested, the perspectives of
the immediate post World War II period were such as to
encourage a brief revival of Clark's emphasis: upon newly
inevitable ups and downs. Quickly thereafter, the
sustained economic growth of postwar America reestablished
interpretative attitudes perhaps more reminiscent of the
1920's than of intervening years. Since recent postwar
prosperity has been founded upon Keynesian policy, the
limitations of Keynes' understanding of the thirties has
hardly seemed fascinating to economists. And Keynes'
theoretical structure was broad and capacious enough to
live on and develop, embracing all sorts of immediate
interpretative needs. Nonetheless, the frightening
dynamic reverses of the American interwar years call for a
virtual methodology of their own. The new and American
conception of Clark probably most closely filled the need.

At the outset, in the American 1920's, three great
traditions were undergoing rapid development and complicated interaction: neo-classical laissez-faire economics;
the younger but tenacious attitudes of American "institutionalism"; and the new orientation to business cycle
analysis. By the 1920's the interpenetration had gone
far enough so that a new context for the consideration of
economic matters was discernable. Neo-classical or
"equilibrium" economics, still built on the assumption

(Say's Law) that general economic activity tended inherently
toward equilibrium at prosperous levels, seemed increasingly
subject to qualification. Institutionalism, in fact, was
most easily understood as a grouping of newer disciplines--
sociological, cultural, and psychological--which were being
used to invade economics and wrest it from nineteenth
century mechanistic bases. The heart of the institutionalist perception was a searching pragmatic relativism, a
notion that man and his environment interacted and evolved
in a process which was not susceptible to formalistic analysis into segmented fields of study. In economics, this
impulse worked to lay bare the social institutions and
habits which contrived in reality to overcome any smoothly
operating economic laws. The purely critical possibilities
of such a view were great, of course, and best embodied in
the work of Thorstein Veblen. He pictured the institutions of a business-dominated society not as automatically
fostering economic progress, but as thwarting it in the
name of profits. Veblen's was an extreme position, but
the institutionalist orientation was commonly bound to an
anti-big-business attitude by the end of the Progressive
period.[1]

---

[1]Cf. Allan G. Gruchy, Modern Economic Thought: The
American Contribution (New York, 1947), Introduction, 1-28.

Yet the tension between institutionalism and neo-classical economics was not incapable of resolution through one or another form of compromise. And there was evidence by the 1920's that the business cycle orientation would offer a fertile field for synthesis. The idea that the capitalist economy was innately cyclical (hence alternately efficient and inefficient) was being pressed by several European, especially Continental, economists after the turn of the century.[2] By the 1920's, Wesley Mitchell was not only a world-renowned cycle analyst, but the most influential economist of America. Yet, as will be seen in a brief chapter on the twenties, the neo-orthodox synthesis developed by the cycle analysts remained very loose and tentative. Various permutations and combinations of the basically institutionalist conception and the equilibrium tradition were possible, which were not deeply oriented to cyclical matters per se. And the sustained prosperity of the twenties finally succeeded in launching a new kind of uncritical or equilibrium-oriented institutionalism. Mitchell himself became increasingly forgetful of potentialities for cyclical depression, as he was impressed by the growing sophistication of business institutions,

[2]For discussion of these backgrounds, cf. Alvin H. Hansen, Business Cycles and National Income (New York, 1964), Part III.

and the staying-power of overall competitive equilibrium.
Thus, when the Depression struck, the elements of the
going synthesis would have to be importantly rearranged.

As will be discussed, Clark's progress during the
1920's had suited him well for the task of reconstruction.
This was certainly so, if the earlier tendency toward
synthesis via strictly cyclical conception was to prove
dominant again. This did occur; it would be fair to say
that the central and unifying endeavor of economic thought
since 1930 has been the study of the business cycle. Yet
great disagreement has persisted--as to whether severe
depressions (especially the Great Depression) are primarily
cyclical events; and as to the precise causes of the
ordinary business cycle. The major writers on the Depression
in the early thirties were largely adherents of the same
neo-orthodoxy of business cycle theory: Mitchell, Hansen,
Schumpeter, and Clark (who was crossing over from institutionalism to cycle theory). Yet their views of the nature
of the cycle were so different that we will be forced to
refer to Schumpeter and Hansen (in the early thirties) as
bulwarks of quasi-conservative orthodoxy, Mitchell as
representative of the flexible neo-orthodoxy of the
twenties, and Clark as distinctly unorthodox. The extent
of their differences was not clear until the intensity of
the Depression drove them not merely to interpret but to

recommend policy (and Schumpeter and Hansen clung to pro-
business laissez-faire).

The American 1920's--or the "New Era," as optimistic business-oriented circles came to call it--had been
more productive, as a period of peaceful interpenetration
of ideas, than appeared from the viewpoint of the early
thirties. From the longer retrospect, it may be argued
that the economists of the New Era were groping for the
same unruffled admixture of equilibrium, institutionalist,
and cyclical concepts that governs professional attitudes
today. The twenties, of course, had not yet built a
secure basis in government policy for such a contented
pluralism. We have built that basis, but only by chance,
and by the deus ex machina of military spending. This
should help us to tolerate whatever laxity attached to
economic ideas during the "New Era." It should, perhaps,
also sober any instinctive attraction we may feel for the
strictly critical economic observers of the early thirties.
Rexford Tugwell will provide the handsomest example of
this group, which carried the tradition of Veblen forward
into the crisis. Whatever the moral veracity of such
thinkers, their increasingly practical and reformist ambi-
tions led them away from the intensively analytic mode of
Veblen. As Arthur Schlesinger Jr. has generalized, the
needs of economic analysis swiftly undermined the sway

which neo-Progressive, neo-institutionalist ideas enjoyed in the early thirties.[3] Only Clark, of the adherents to explicitly critical institutionalism, found ways of keeping the attention of the economics profession at large. He did this not by reasserting the general sense of Veblen and proposing social reconstruction, as Tugwell did--but by carrying business cycle theory to the point at which it embodied a more shocking critique than institutionalism could muster.[4]

In certain respects, Clark may be seen to have brought to a surprising climax the views of Simon Patten, rather than to have developed the larger institutionalist perception per se. Patten had imported into economics, during the Progressive period, the seminal American perspective by which economic questions might be viewed in the

---

[3]Cf. Schlesinger's introduction to Seymour Harris, ed., American Economic History (New York, 1961), 20-21.

[4]The most important secondary work on institutionalism in America is Allan G. Gruchy, Modern Economic Thought: The American Contribution. He gives fuller accounts of the thought of Clark, Mitchell, Tugwell, Commons, and Means than we have space to give. Our general exception to his work is that he binds these men too closely together, as representatives of a common tradition. At least for our purposes--study of the interpretation of the 1920's and 1930's--they must be more sharply distinguished: Clark in particular, but Mitchell importantly too.

A more concise, flexible, and suggestive reference work is the set of essays (including excellent ones by Joseph Dorfman, Simon Kuznets, and Robert A. Gordon): Institutional Economics (Berkeley, 1963).

context of material abundance or "surplus" rather than the classical assumption of scarcity. With this emphasis went an orientation to consumption, and to the problems of planning for its enhancement. Tugwell was the closest thing to an explicit disciple of Patten, merging his ideas with Veblen's during the 1920's and later. Yet the 1920's saw so rapid a spread of preoccupation with abundance, and levels of consumption, that the prior insights of Patten might be considered already to have reached an influential maturity. Patten's concern with social planning for abundant consumption, representing the most ambitious and optimistic side of American institutionalism, attained the status of a liberal orthodoxy by the early New Deal years. Sadly, the distinctive contributions of Patten had been fully absorbed, without important results for the interpretation of the great cycle of 1921-1933. It was Clark, from the twenties onward, who brought the orientation to consumption into tight synthesis with the dominant investment-based schools of business cycle theory, in his concept of the "acceleration principle." While supposed heirs of Patten such as Tugwell were increasingly pushed to under-consumptionist analyses of the crisis, Clark worked for a formulation that would integrate the untrammelled abundance of the twenties with the dynamic reversal of the thirties. Only such an economics could render Patten's legacy continuingly and strictly germane to America.[5]

---

[5]On Patten, see Daniel M. Fox, <u>The Discovery of</u>
<u>Abundance, Simon N. Patten and the Transformation of</u>
<u>Social Theory</u> (Ithaca, 1967). Fox does not overestimate
the importance of the idea of "abundance" for American
social thought; it was, however, too general to aid
economic analysis <u>per</u> <u>se</u> very greatly. Fox is correct
that there was an important affinity between some of
Keynes' perspectives and Patten's. But we will discuss
these in connection with the weaker points of Keynesian
analysis—by which abundance was seen in an absolutistic
way, as "surplus" and as a barrier to further progress.
We shall come to the conclusion that Clark best approximated a truly relative concept of abundance, adequate to
the extremes of American prosperity and Depression.

CHAPTER I

THE NEW ERA SYNTHESIS ON THE
EVE OF THE ONSLAUGHT

To view the scene most generally, the American
twenties were a time which yielded a notable degree of
accommodation between orthodox economics and the critical-
historical school of institutionalism. There was an ever
more widely diffused feeling among economists in the "New
Era" that the classical mechanisms for prosperous equilibrium could not be relied upon and "let alone": there
was also required a kind of economic management--in the
corporation and in government agencies--that was not
mrely shrewd but creative. In this sense, the critique of
capitalist institutions had been absorbed, and even more
so, the institutionally-oriented approach to economics.
Of course, institutionalists of various sorts commonly proposed radical reorganization of the system, while the other
economists were content to urge improvement of the policies
of management and government under the existing structure
of capitalism. But, on either hand, the Deweyite impulse
toward rationally directed social progress had been loosed
in economics. The twenties have been called an apolitical

age enamored of the cruder powers of the economic world. This is true, but in the case of the economists themselves, politicizing or institutionalizing tendencies were unprecedentedly strong.[1]

The tradition of institutionalism itself underwent substantial dilution in terms of its critical content. Veblen's last great contribution, Absentee Ownership (1923), was never to be matched in the systematic fury of its critique. There Veblen pictured an interlocking capitalist regime of diabolical intent and omnipotent control. For the sole end of guaranteeing a consistent return on the capital of its absentee owners, business had replaced classical price competition with mere sales competition, instituted low wages and permanent unemployment, and set up a policy of severe restriction of production. The resultant secular trend described by Veblen would yield diminishing levels of consumption and the decay of technology itself, as capital and labor selfishly--even consciously--warred to make their services scarcer and less productive.[2] Yet, as American capitalism moved from

_____

[1] For an introduction to the dedication to social improvement which held sway during the twenties in most academic disciplines, see the superb article, Henry F. May, "Shifting Perspectives on the 1920's," Miss. Valley Historical Review, v. 43, Dec. 1956, 405-427.

[2] Thorstein Veblen, Absentee Ownership and Business Enterprise in Recent Times (New York, 1923), 398-445.

the death-rattling of 1919-21 to the prolonged prosperity
and social harmony of the later twenties, the views of
dominant writers in the critical tradition left those of
Veblen far behind.

For the economists of the New Era were increasingly setting forth, whether in subtle accents or bold,
perspectives that represented a perfect inversion of
Veblen's conception. The resources of capitalist management and its governmental adjuncts such as the Federal
Reserve were indeed seen as potent--but for expansion and
prosperity. Corporations were considered to be improving
technology at a remarkable rate, holding prices stable as
costs were reduced, and paying high wages to support a
rising consumption. The trend toward combination itself
was looked upon in a positive light: mergers and trade
associations promoted technology, concentrated capital use-
fully, and in general strengthened the potential of business for progressive policy. Even the business cycle,
which at first appeared to be the peculiar object of
critical concern for economists of the twenties, was more
and more thought to be yielding to the new expertise.

The last important general study of the economy
before the Collapse, written by an economist in the
critical tradition, was Columbia Professor Rexford
Tugwell's Industry's Coming of Age of 1927. Influenced by

Veblen, as well as the more explicit concern with social
planning in the work of Simon Patten, Tugwell embodied
the full range of attitudes implied by the concept
"institutionalism." But more than this, Tugwell's work
demonstrated the power with which New Era notions were
distracting the critical tradition. The greater part of
the _Coming of Age_ was caught up in a fascinated enumeration of the factors that had made for large gains in productivity since the War. The general causes ranged from
increased employment of women to improved levels of edu-
cation; but prominent among them were industrial combination and containment of the trade cycle. Tugwell
described both combination and trade association as having
enhanced managerial efficiency, technical sophistication,
and coordination of supply to demand.[3] This latter result
bore on the improved stability of the economy, but Tugwell
saw other factors besides combination as having moderated
the cycle.[4] The Federal Reserve's control over credit
conditions was one factor. But the major influence
adduced by Tugwell, in a moment of the most naive sort of
New Era enthusiasm, was increased knowledge of the cycle
and of statistics bearing on the cycle. If business could

---

[3]Rexford Tugwell, _Industry's Coming of Age_ (New
York, 1927), 110-114.

[4]_Ibid._, 93-97.

anticipate depression, ". . . it simply would not happen, because of the preparation for it which would immediately occur."[5] Yet, under whatever economic theory, Tugwell would have made as much sense by holding that the "preparations" would involve dangerous cutbacks.

Later Tugwell dealt with wage policy. Here he made a full concession to what was perhaps the most important single New Era doctrine. He stated that a high wage policy had won over business; that wage reductions were a thing of the past; that these things importantly bolstered consumption. At the same time labor, as in the 1925 pronouncement of the A.F.L., had gone over to a high productivity policy. Tugwell, in a fulsome New Era fashion, viewed higher wages and higher productivity as mutually reinforcing trends in the contemporary economy.[6]

Finally, late in the study, Tugwell treated the "barriers to productivity," reasserting the older sort of institutionalist critique and leaving behind the institutionalism of the New Era. Some of the "barriers," however, such as the mediocrity of educational standards and the business cycle, he had already discussed differently, as

---

[5]Ibid., 94.

[6]Ibid., 191-195. Schlesinger appears to have misread Tugwell, claiming that he charged industry with a low wage policy. Cf. Schlesinger, Crisis of the Old Order (Cambridge, Mass., 1957), 195.

recently yielding to amelioration. It was, of course, a
mark of large-mindedness that he was ready to discuss
factors both as having improved and as urgently needing
further improvement. But it was also a mark of ambivalence,
and of the power with which New Era notions were at work in
Tugwell. Still and all, he moved to an emphatic conclusion,
roundly Veblenite and brazenly instrumentalist. Despite
great gains in efficiency and production, the economic
system could yield, after full governmental restructuring,
far greater gains. With a change of "social rules,"
industry would be "greatly pleased to double the amount of
goods it turns out within a month."[7]

Tugwell's most critical emphases emerged in conjunction with his proposals for reform. He argued that
governmental control must be exercised in the essential
areas of capital allocation and price policy. He held,
a propos of the former, that certain industries (such as
textiles and coal) had been laggard in modernizing plant.[8]
With greater vehemence, Tugwell charged that a more common
fault of industry was its tendency to reinvest profits,
rather than to distribute them as dividends. Hence there
had come into being an "enormous overequipment of every

---

[7]Tugwell, ibid., 241.

[8]Ibid., 208-211.

one of our great industries."[9] Passing from the critique
of parsimonious and backward industries, to the indictment
of lavish overinvestment--Tugwell simply reversed himself.
It might be said that the notions of Patten were softening
and readjusting the harshest emphases of Veblen's critique.
Moreover, as Tugwell went on to discuss the need for price
control, he gave more ground than Veblen (to whom the
capitalist price system always remained a bête noire). At
first Tugwell stated the theme with a vigor worthy of the
master, or of the revived institutionalist polemics of the
1930's. He maintained that as business grows larger it
tends to cease sharing with the consumer, through lower
prices, the fruits of technological progress: business
starts restricting output and keeping prices high. Yet
Tugwell abruptly backtracked, by granting that in the
1920's most of the great combinations were still young,
still coordinating prices to falling costs of production.
In this matter he especially lauded (with most commentators
in the twenties) the automobile industry. Tugwell brought
the case to a consistent enough conclusion: he warned that
corporate power seemed to be nearing the point at which
abusive price policies became likely.[10] His argument was

---

[9]Ibid., 236.

[10]Ibid., 157-159, 236.

suggestive, but the captains of New Era industry were exonerated for the time being.

Industry's Coming of Age was conceived precisely in the spirit of its title. The managed--well managed--capitalism of the 1920's was seen as a necessary, constructive stage preparatory to the full centralization and rationalization of the economy. The heady extrapolations into the future were almost as much a variety of New Era enthusiasm as of institutionalist criticism. It would not be enough to point out that Tugwell had been a disciple of Patten as well as of Veblen, and that the former's views were generally more optimistic. Tugwell's analysis of the economic scene was, for the most part, broadly representative of New Era conception. It was also, of course, a flexible enough analysis and program so that in the Depression Tugwell could carry forward his views without far-reaching changes. But there would be notable difficulties: for example, Tugwell's acceptance in 1927 of the idea of decreasing cyclicality.

Wesley C. Mitchell, the uncontested authority on cycles in America by the 1920's, would have more striking difficulties. Mitchell's accommodation to New Era modes of thought had been rather more uniform than Tugwell's. The presiding spirit of the National Bureau of Economic Research through the twenties, as well as Professor at

Columbia, Mitchell was the embodiment of the hopeful colla-
boration of academic economics and government. Mitchell's
views had come to represent more than any other's the
standard of economic neo-orthodoxy in the twenties. Originally inspired by Veblen, Mitchell had soon been drawn into
a purely empirical and quantitative approach to economics.
He established himself by a volume in 1913 as the most
painstaking student of measurable economic fluctuations.[11]
Aloofness from theoretical bias, whether of institutionalism
or of neo-classical tradition, inevitably characterized his
efforts. He had proposed piecemeal government controls for
stabilizing the cycle in his work of 1913, but evinced little
interest in overall economic reconstruction from that time
until 1932. At the latter date, Mitchell partly reverted
to radical criticism and socialistic proposals. But in
1929 he wrote the definitive document of moderate New Era
economics.[12]

---

[11]Wesley C. Mitchell, Business Cycles (Berkeley,
1913). His later large work was Business Cycles--The
Problem and its Setting (New York, 1927). On Mitchell's
empirical detachment, see Simon Kuznets, "The Contribution
of Wesley C. Mitchell," in Institutional Economics
(Berkeley, 1963).

[12]Cf. Allan G. Gruchy, Modern Economic Thought:
The American Contribution (New York, 1947), 303-307.
Gruchy, interested in developing the institutionalist
aspects of Mitchell's career, does not treat this essay.

This was his summarizing essay in the two-volume National Bureau Report on the 1920's economy.[13] Mitchell's "Review" was the Report's last word, written by remarkable coincidence just a half year before the Crash of late 1929. Mitchell was temperate, and critical in many places, but essentially optimistic. No finer index could be found for the bases of optimism in the New Era than this essay, passionately objective but written without the aids to hindsight afforded by the Depression. On most of the large issues Mitchell shunned the simpler slogans of the New Era. At the outset he urged that the twenties represented the general process of industrialization, and not something conceptually new.[14] He did not hesitate to describe the overall domestic situation as "a queer mixture of prosperity and depression." But in his interpretation of this situation he adduced as basic causes "indirect and direct competition" between more and less rapidly advancing sectors of the economy.[15] And he stressed that the severest restraint on overall expansion, in industry and agriculture, was economic and price weakness abroad.[16] No

---

[13] President's Conference on Unemployment (Report of), Recent Economic Changes (New York, 1929).

[14] Ibid., v. 2, 842.

[15] Ibid., 867.

[16] Ibid., 857, 884, 909.

sign here of the older institutionalist critique of the suffocation of competition or the bloating of capitalist organization. In fact, Mitchell was concerned lest corporate profits run too low: bigness of industry he saw as no defense against the forces of international price weakness, or domestic competition _via_ advancing technology. These things were reducing the profit rates in some industries, regardless of size, to inhibiting levels.[17]

He fully adverted to the difficulties of agriculture, particularly its burden of debts. Yet he considered the farmers to have reattained their prewar relative income status by 1925, and asserted that with continued prosperity agriculture would "work its way out" of remaining difficulties.[18] As to unemployment, Mitchell put its rate at 5-6% (1923-27), and deplored it as too high. But he described it as largely "technological," and representing temporary sacrifice for future advances in productivity.[19] Such was his cautious and balanced optimism. It was not until he treated labor that he unblushingly embraced the New Era. The high wage-high consumption doctrine he endorsed as successful in theory

---

[17]_Ibid._, 873-874.

[18]_Ibid._, 883, 909.

[19]_Ibid._, 876-878.

and in practice. He considered its institution as largely
fortuitous--the postwar deflation of 1920-21 had seen
prices decline relative to wages. Business, he somewhat
excitedly held, had at that time come to see the advantages
of a high wage policy, and had not much hesitated to pursue
it. Equally earnest priase was given labor for its
complementary policy of high productivity. Mitchell rather
marvelled that the high wage policy could move forward
under the current conditions of fairly low profits and
declining prices. But he saw no doubt that the policy
was, simply, working: consumption was increasing in proportion to expanded output of consumers goods.[20] Mitchell,
like Tugwell only more unqualifiedly, subscribed to the
cardinal tenet of New Era economics.

The more extravagant claim of some New Era writers,
that the business cycle had been "ironed out," Mitchell
professed to doubt. Yet he conceded this as a possibility, and corroborated the fact that short cyclical movements since 1921 had been less pronounced than before.
Mitchell went on to argue that it was too early to discuss
the fate of the cycle in general--for should European
demand, and hence American agriculture, strongly revive,
then "our skill in controlling cycles will be put to a

---

[20]Ibid., 864-866, 875.

severer test." For now, he asserted that since there had
been no "unhealthy boom" it was naturally unlikely that
there would have been any "violent relapse." Addressing
the outlook in the spring of 1929, Mitchell did note,
mainly with reference to stock market speculation, "signs
that the caution inspired by that disastrous year [1921]
is wearing thin." He expressed some doubt that "progress
in the arts of industry and business" could maintain
unabated its recent brisk pace. But it was clear that
Mitchell considered the threat of overbuilding and overspeculation to be potential rather than actual in the
spring of 1929.[21]

Whether prosperity would endure depended, for
Mitchell, simply upon the continued application of "intelligence." Where he generalized on the economic success of
the twenties--in the face of foreign stagnation--he gave
the credit to intelligence. He meant to include all the
applications of economic intelligence, technical and
organizational. He felt, as noted above, that wage policy
and labor relations had seen focal enlightenment during
the decade. But Mitchell did not fail to add praise for
the other efforts of management, including shared intelligence through trade associations, and for the policies of

---

[21]Ibid., 893, 909-910.

the various governmental agencies as well.[22] While
Mitchell urged that the entire industrial revolution has
been a history of the uses of intelligence, it was evident
that he viewed its latest stage as embodying a heightened
exercise of that old virtue.

The great National Bureau Report with its conclusion by Mitchell, despite whatever intended detachment,
became a bulwark of late New Era opinion. It was appealed
to as an ultimate authority by Professor Irving Fisher of
Yale, who has come to seem almost synonomous with New Era
complacency. Fisher was the most highly reputed academic
monetary theorist of America, as well as one of the most
inventive expositors of the new prosperity. He was much
discussed for his proposals on price stabilization; and by
1925 he had spiritedly denied that the "so-called business
cycle" had any essential basis in the economic system.[23]
Fisher's book of 1930, The Stock Market Crash--And After,
was a bold effort to reformulate optimism, concerning both
the stock market and the economy at large. As to the
latter, he did not greatly elaborate his arguments, pre-
ferring simply to refer his readers to the National Bureau

---

[22]Ibid., 862-866, 910.

[23]Cf. Irving Fisher, "Our Unstable Dollar and the
So-Called Business Cycle," Journal of the American
Statistical Association, v. 20, June 1925, 179-202.

Report. Speaking generally, Fisher characterized the
economy of the 1920's as highly "dynamic"; he pointed to
the rapid rate of technical advance, the growing expertise
of business management (including the policy of mergers),
the cooperative policy of labor, and the healthy, stable
price level. He claimed to disdain cruder assertions that
a wholly New Era was upon us, but reiterated the notion of
the Report that an "intensification" of economic development was taking place.[24] This concept had been most firmly
urged in the Introduction to the Report, signed by the
sponsoring Committee on Recent Economic Changes (including
business figures such as John J. Raskob, and Owen Young,
along with President Hoover himself). Their satisfaction
may have affected the introduction, but its concept was
perfectly compatible with Mitchell's view.[25]

In most respects Mitchell's notion of the intensity of progress was more qualified than Fisher's, or
Hoover's. In one sense, however, it went further--
Mitchell considered competitive advance to have been so
strenuous as to threaten profits in some industries. This
concern with profits, in turn, represented the only difference in kind between Fisher's analysis and Mitchell's.

---

[24]Fisher, The Stock Market Crash--And After (New
York, 1930), 100.

[25]Recent Economic Changes, Introduction p. IX.

Fisher's book centered on the stock market, and on the argument that since corporate earnings had been high, stock prices had risen not through mad speculation but through rational reappraisal of the earning power of companies. In any case, Mitchell's concern with the weaker industries did not seem ultimately to conflict with Fisher's orientation: for we have seen that Mitchell did not discern large overspeculation in early 1929. Interestingly, Fisher, in retrospect, allowed that early 1929 had seen too great a rise in stock prices relative to current earnings. He went on to say that the subsequent boom in profits had corrected this maladjustment by September, even before the Crash.[26] Judging from Mitchell's methodology, one might assume that the profit boom in the months after his review would have allayed many of his doubts (both on profits and on speculation), and landed him squarely in Fisher's boat.

Fisher felt that Hoover's program of the winter of 1929-30 would be sufficient to overcome tendencies toward depression that might have been unleashed by the Crash. Fisher voiced certain anxieties: about "saturation" in the fields of building and autos, about the possibility of gold shortage and long-term price deflation, and, most of all, about a potential psychological blow to investment due to

---

[26]Fisher, _Crash_, 84-90.

the Crash. But none of these seemed terribly ominous to
Fisher; and the worst of them, the last, seemed amenable
to Hoover's approach. Hoover was working to maintain both
investment and consumption, and nothing more seemed
required.[27] Further, Fisher could appeal to Mitchell, whom
he quoted as of December 1929: Hoover's actions comprised
an "[extremely] significant experiment in the technique of
balance."[28]

"Balance"--cultivated and heightened by social
intelligence. This was the New Era synthesis and transformation of classical equilibrium concepts and the institutionalist impulse. The new equilibrium was institutionally maintained, rather than automatically achieved by
classical competitive mechanisms. In fact, these mechanisms were coming to be seen as something of a disruptive
factor in the equation of balance. Mitchell, while denying
Veblen's thesis that competition had been sacrificed for
stability, did seem to view the forces of competition with
apprehension--as potentially deranging and depressing
influences upon prices and profits. He also, of course,
saw competition as a vital concomitant of progress, and as
successfully collaborating in the complex balance of the

[27]Ibid., 58, 64, 268-269.

[28]Ibid., 24.

twenties. But Mitchell, however tentatively, was contributing to a fascinating New Era emphasis. This was the
replacement of competitive equilibrium by high-wage and
consumption equilibrium. Prosperous economic balance
would be insured by rising levels of consumption, not by
price-depressing competition.

This development was not quite a matter of explicit
doctrine, but was a clear conceptual tendency. As it
appeared to sap the strength of the older institutionalist
critique, a newer, more germane critical impulse made itself
felt. This was underconsumptionism, as popularized in
America by Foster and Catchings (an ex-president of Reed
College, and a business man). Their approach clearly
paralleled New Era thinking--only they doubted that consumption could be raised fast enough to retain balance,
unless more concentrated policies (such as higher government
spending) were devised.[29] During the early Depression the
institutionalist critique was revived with a more explicit
underconsumptionist focus than it had possessed. Hence the
dominant liberal interpretations of the Depression often
amounted to little more than protestations that the New Era

---

[29]Cf. William Trufant Foster and Waddill Catchings,
Business Without a Buyer (Boston, 1927), 8-37. For a fine
and sympathetic sketch of their outlook, see Schlesinger,
Crisis of the Old Order, 134-136. We shall refer to them
again below.

had not practiced what it preached: wages had <u>not</u> been
raised enough, prices had <u>not</u> fallen enough, and so on.
Then too, a fully articulated orthodox critique grew up,
which held that the New Era had indeed done too much:
wages had gone too high, government had meddled too much,
etc. These matters will be discussed in the next chapter.
They provide evidence of the depth of the impression made
by characteristic New Era attitudes upon the economic mind.

These attitudes, oriented toward the reinforcement
of classical equilibrium through institutional aids and
policies, played their major intellectual role in providing
correctives for apprehension concerning the business cycle.
The field of business cycle analysis was young but highly
ambitious. The very men, such as Mitchell, who had so
recently established the general character of the cycle,
were already leaders in the effort to overcome its influence. That the cycle existed had seemed the greatest single
concession of economic thought to the tradition of criticism
of capitalist institutions from Marx onward. And the imposition of institutional correctives to the cycle seemed
destined to put a period to an epochal dialogue. The
severity of the Depression, however, would underscore the
areas of confusion that still marked business cycle theory
itself.

The problem of cycles, and of other changes in the
level of economic activity, was often referred to in the

twenties as the problem of "dynamic" economics. John
Maurice Clark (who will be discussed separately in
Chapter III) urged that classical static equilibrium analysis must be replaced by a new and "dynamic" set of assumptions. But even in the use of the word, the prejudices
and confusions of the twenties made themselves felt. As
seen above, Fisher used the term "dynamic" to denote the
potency of innovation and growth during the decade.
Clark's essay on dynamics of 1927 manifested ambiguities
of its own. On the one hand, Clark used "dynamic" almost
as a synonym for the institutionalist orientation--evolu-
tionary, complex, realistic--opposing these qualities to the
abstract, timeless, and lawful nature of orthodox
economics.[30] On the other hand, Clark outlined far more
specifically economic-analytical uses for the term. In
particular he stressed the idea of "cumulative" economic
changes over against the characteristic "self-limiting"
mechanisms of equilibrium theory.[31] The cumulative, or

---

[30]John M. Clark, "The Relations Between Statics
and Dynamics," Economic Essays, Jacob Hollander ed. (New
York, 1927), 48, 69.
      Gruchy tends to use "dynamic" this way, inter-
changing it with "evolutionary," "holistic," and "institutionalist." We shall use it strictly to denote change-
ability in the general level of economic activity,
especially as in cyclicality. Cf. Gruchy, Economic Thought,
3-4.

[31]Clark, Ibid., 48, 52.

"self-reinforcing" tendencies, however, might play a part
in various sorts of analyses. Fisher, again, had described
a self-reinforcing prosperity. Moreover, Fisher's New Era
emphasis on the role of the enlightened policies of management and labor fitted Clark's more general institutionalist
definition of dynamics as well.

A full theoretical system of cumulative change was
understood to include the contraction phase of the cycle,
as well as expansion. But cycle theory itself had tended
to resist any extremely dynamic formulation. It remained
oriented to equilibrium analysis, simply transforming it
into longer-run conceptions. That is, cycle theories
normally assumed that depression set the stage for revival
at a higher general level of activity than had obtained at
the close of the previous business cycle. A fine study in
the dilemma of cycle theory was provided by the work of
Joseph Schumpeter, a dominant figure since 1911.
Schumpeter argued powerfully that capitalist technological
advance was made in an inherently dynamic way: innovations
came in "swarms" which inevitably touched off first an
investment boom and then depression. During the latter the
economy adapted itself to the new forms of production by
casting out older, uncompetitive forms.[32] Schumpeter saw

---

[32]Joseph Schumpeter, The Theory of Economic Development (Cambridge, Mass., 1934), 216 ff. (First published in
German 1911, revised 1926, translated into English 1934)

this dynamic oscillation as so essential to progress, that
after coming to Harvard in 1932 he became the foremost
deflationist, anti-New Deal economist in America. It seemed
difficult for him to contemplate that depression might fail
to establish a new equilibrium, might not be self-limiting.
The high dynamism of his conception was strongly hedged
about by the reflexes of the classical method.[33]

Leader as he was in cycle theory, then, Schumpeter
would stand largely for orthodoxy in the thirties. Spokesmen of the economic optimism of the 1920's, who labored for

---

[33]It should be evident that Schumpeter's investment based theory of cycles drew its dynamic not only from
technological history (one thinks of Veblen), but from the
competitive institutional structure of capitalism (seen as
still more intensely functioning than in classical theory).
Both wings of the construct may be seen as institutionalist permutations of classical theory, for the objectives
of dynamic business cycle theory. Schumpeter himself
sprang from the late nineteenth century German schools of
history, which embodied the major non-American parallel to
institutionalism, and an early influence upon it. For a
superb description of Schumpeter-as-institutionalist,
which argues that he was only clearly an un-American
institutionalist in the vast historical compass of his work
(as culminated in 1939 and 1942)--see Robert A. Gordon,
"Institutional Elements in Contemporary Economics," in
Institutional Economics (Berkeley, 1963), 141-147.
(Schumpeter's olympian determinism, and lack of faith in
reformist efforts, Gordon compares with similar traits of
Veblen.) For our part, we hope later to treat
Schumpeter with fullest respect, as indeed the "Marx" of
the entire half century prior to 1925 or so. There have
been other Marxes: Veblen in the American Progressive
period at least; but even more so, we think, Clark in the
Interwar Era in America.

control of the cycle, had in some senses less dynamic ways
of conceiving matters. Their desire to control the cycle
seemed linked to a weakening of their faith in self-limiting mechanisms. Yet their confidence that stability could
be managed argued an underestimation of the dynamic potential of the economy. Some tended to see the cycle in ways
less oriented to the movements of basic investment, and more
to ancillary disturbances in the realm of finance. The
Englishman Ralph Hawtrey, a leading cycle analyst, was
sanguine by 1926 that if credit could continue to be controlled judiciously, it would be found that the cycle had
been banished.[34] Fisher's views were similar. Others, such
as Mitchell, took a studiously eclectic approach, searching,
as shown above, investment, consumption, prices, profits,
and finance for signs of imbalance. Mitchell eyed all
deflationary tendencies nervously. But (despite his
sympathy with Schumpeter's concept of depression-from-
competition) he simply was not armed with a highly dynamic
conception of the cycle.

With the coming of the Great Depression, the hopeful synthesis of equilibrium economics and the

---

[34]Ralph G. Hawtrey, "The Trade Cycle," reprinted in
Readings in Business Cycle Theory, American Economic
Association (Philadelphia, 1944), 333-349. (Originally
published 1926 in a Dutch journal.)

institutionalist orientation--centering in the field of cycle theory and control--was dashed apart. Where emphasis had gradually been drawn to the cultivation of a dynamic growth, now blind contraction carried all before it. If the whole period had been the result of some newly dynamic cyclical cause, prevalent cycle theory was in no state immediately to comprehend it. New synthesis would have to wait on dismemberment of the old.

CHAPTER II

THE REACTION AGAINST NEW ERA CONCEPTION

The evident failure of both the analyses and the
policies of the New Era gave rise to a furious effort at
revision, but to an often facile one. The frailty of
equilibrium was, in the Contraction, so profoundly felt
that every critical nuance seemed trenchant, seemed to
touch a dynamic problem. Hence, in a sense, progress
toward fundamental advance in cycle theory was blocked by
the very profusion of interpretative activity. The orthodox and unorthodox economists moved swiftly into contradiction so flat as to suggest glibness and bias. The neo-
orthodoxy of the 1920's (including Mitchell and Fisher)
seemed to feel a greatly heightened sense of the instability of the economy, but a new cautiousness in describing
its inner workings. Finally, on all sides, there was an
inevitable redoubling of preoccupation with questions of
economic policy per se. For example, leaders of radical
and neo-institutionalist thought, by the time of Roosevelt's
accession, were already preparing for full social reconstruction rather than scholarly analysis. With all groups seek-
ing to direct policy, an atmosphere was created which

-36-

amounted to a virtual apotheosis of the New Era orientation toward the management of economic institutions. By the same token, destructive criticism of the policies of the 1920's was essential to all forms of interpretation. Paradox seemed the order of the day. No wonder the New Deal itself ultimately embodied a very strained synthesis of underconsumptionist and monopolistic concepts, a kind of grandiose and re-fabricated New Era.

Among the variants of neo-institutionalist and underconsumptionist critique, the boldest inversion of New Era argument was put forward by Foster and Catchings by early 1931. They used recent statistics to enhance their earlier description of underconsumption. They stated simply that from 1900 to 1925 productivity had risen 54% while real wages had risen only 30%. That AFL policy had turned toward the adjustment of wages to productivity in 1925 they considered a necessary move that had come too late to stave off a developing crisis of underconsumption and overinvestment.[1] The very wage policy that the New Era had seen as a vital innovation, Foster found almost entirely absent--and to its absence he single-mindedly laid the severity of the Depression. This construction, so

---

[1] W. Foster and W. Catchings, "Must We Reduce Our Standard of Living?" Forum, v. 85, February 1931, 75-77.

partial in its analysis of the flow of purchasing power, and so clearly an evolution of New Era thought, was to become a cornerstone of liberal criticism.

George Soule, influential as the editor of the New Republic and as an analyst of economic affairs, expanded the critique of the New Era along similar lines in his book of 1932, A Planned Society. Unlike Foster, Soule wrote to promote full structural rather than fiscal reform. But his interpretative stance was flatly underconsumptionist: that overcapacity of industry and relative lack of purchasing power were the issues, he considered so obvious as to be "trite."[2] He explained that in the 1920's wages had not risen enough, and prices had not fallen enough, to clear the market of the vast output made possible by technological advance. Installment credit had temporarily made up the deficit in buying power, and when it reached its limits so ended the New Era myth of cyclical stability in a "mature" economy.[3]

In criticizing the role of rigid prices in bringing on the Depression, Soule connected with the key emphasis of the revived institutionalist critique of the early thirties.

---

[2]George Soule, A Planned Society (New York, 1932), 66.

[3]Ibid., 26.

The academic institutionalists, such as Tugwell and
Gardiner Means, were moving toward the underconsumptionism
of Foster and Soule: but in a gingerly way. In fact
their entire effort to interpret the Great Cycle was
extremely limited. Tugwell's large work of 1933, The
Industrial Discipline, was organized to demonstrate the
practical possibilities for social control of production.
In this context Tugwell merely restated, with more elaboration, his 1927 proposals for central control of prices and
capital allocation. These two wings of his approach were
somewhat more explicitly unified now, and oriented to purchasing power. He considered overhead costs from overbuilt
and badly allocated capital to put upward pressure on
prices; high prices in turn to mulct the consumer and
restrict production. Competition was carried out more
through sales pressure than through price reduction.[4]
Oddly, no other interpretative themes were treated; and
the problem of the business cycle itself was not mentioned!
It is clear that Tugwell considered the task before him to
be planning for reconstruction rather than close analysis
of the Collapse. After all, he had favored full revamping
of the institutions of capitalism even when they were, in
his own description, functioning rather well.

[4]Tugwell, The Industrial Discipline and the
Governmental Arts (New York, 1933), 180, 186, 204.

After beginning his practical involvement in the New Deal recovery program, Tugwell addressed himself more explicitly to the causes of the severity of the Depression. His book had considered general failings of the system; now in an article of 1934 Tugwell attempted to explain the new cyclicality, which he had missed in 1927 and failed to consider in 1933. He focused on the role of the price system, rigid in industry and flexible in agriculture. The reflex of industry after the onset of depression had been to hold prices rigid, cut production, and disemploy labor, thus curtailing consumer purchasing power. At the same time agriculture had kept production high, greatly lowered prices, and hence also experienced diminished purchasing power. The intensification of the Depression had been brought about by a vicious circle of decreasing consumption by farmers and labor.[5] (Tugwell went on to present and endorse the New Deal plan to raise farm prices and income, and to raise industrial production and employment.)

The older Veblenian critique of rigidity and over-stabilization was rendered more dynamic, then, through development of its latent affinities for underconsumption-ism. Interestingly, this conception did not necessarily

---

[5] Tugwell, "The Price Also Rises," *Fortune*, v. 9, January 1934, 71-72, 107-108.

imply that underconsumption or other distortions had
specially risen during the New Era years. Tugwell's new
conception was a plausible extension of his 1927 work,
where current economic balance was granted but suspicion
was expressed over the potential mismanagement of the price
system. Yet the extremity of the economic crisis argued an
extremity of abuse in the price system, under this interpretation, that was not really explained or even argued in
Tugwell's book of 1933 or his article of 1934.

Unquestionably Tugwell's confidence in the efficacy
of his interpretation had been bolstered by the éclat of
the volume The Modern Corporation and Private Property by
Gardiner Means and Adolf Berle, published in 1933. Means
was a young Ph.D. in economics, Berle a law professor at
Columbia. Their book has been considered to embody the
scholarly culmination of a generation of institutionalist
inquiry. Yet if Tugwell showed a certain narrowness or
inhibition of interpretative approach, Means and Berle
manifested something close to muteness. They documented
the past and continuing growth of the huge corporation,
with a meticulous emphasis on the divorce of ownership and
control. They asserted in a rough, appended conclusion that
the days of small and classically competitive units were
ended, and with them the tendency toward equilibrium

posited by classical theory.[6] But the book, and Means'
preliminary article of 1931, held no explicit description
or interpretation of the Depression whatsoever.[7] Its
authors indicated in general terms, much in the sense of
Veblen's critique of 1923, that management, no longer
synonymous with ownership, had lost the "initiative"
requisite to capitalist progress.[8] In addition, they made
brief mention of the conditions of high fixed capital and
overhead costs which now pervaded industry.[9] Here they
called to mind the emphasis of John Maurice Clark's
Studies in the Economics of Overhead Costs of 1923, one of
the great works of moderate institutionalist general theory.
That work will be discussed later for its special contributions to dynamic theory in the 1930's. One of its ideas
was to relate large unemployment to the capitalist effort
to protect overhead by reducing wage expenditures in
depression.[10] This was germane to Tugwell's interpretation
of the Depression. Yet he did not develop the matter, and

[6]Adolf A. Berle Jr. and Gardiner C. Means, The
Modern Corporation and Private Property (New York, 1933),
345-351.

[7]Means, "The Large Corporation in American Life,"
American Economic Review, v. 21, March 1931, 10-37.

[8]Means and Berle, Modern Corporation, 347-350.

[9]Ibid., 351.

[10]J. M. Clark, Studies in the Economics of Overhead
Costs (Chicago, 1923), 298-299.

Means and Berle did not put forward any interpretation
into which it might be fitted. They mentioned high overhead costs in conjunction with monopolistic pricing, but
did not relate pricing to cyclical depression.

Means finally, in an article of 1934, explicitly
registered agreement with Tugwell's approach. He asserted,
briefly, that the Depression would have been much less
severe had business maintained production and allowed
prices to fall freely.[11] Later Means and others further
developed the critique of rigid prices.[12] But by then,
other developments in the study of investment and consumption were taking a fairly clear initiative. Nor was
it accidental that the dominant writers in the institutionalist tradition had been laggard and half-hearted in
the realm of concrete interpretation. For this had been
the moment of their accession to political power. Their
tradition had prepared them to accept in quite sweeping
terms the demise of equilibrium and of capitalism: now
was the time to construct something better. Tugwell had
been most forthright in the orientation of his Industrial
Discipline to economic reconstruction rather than to
analysis. And Berle and Means, though centering their

---

[11]Means, "The Consumer and the New Deal," Annals
of the American Academy of Political and Social Science,
v. 173, May 1934, 11.

[12]See below, pp. 138-150.

efforts upon a laborious documentation, gave the work
unity only by a concluding recommendation. The two themes,
concerning the sheer size of the corporation and its irresponsibility to ownership, joined forcefully in suggesting
the need for social control.[13] This large preoccupation
of institutionalism now seemed to embody its central thrust.
Its sheerly critical and interpretative aspects seemed to
atrophy: its interpretation of the Depression came to
little more than an indictment of industrial management's
price policy from 1929-1933.

Viewing as a rough whole the price critique and the
broader underconsumption-overinvestment approach--the left
had mounted a rather full challenge to New Era assumptions.
Yet dissension was to be compounded as certain economists
rose to the attack on the New Era from more orthodox
premises. Following Schumpeter's adaptation of Say's Law
to the business cycle, they generally focused on the
problems of investment rather than of consumption. Theirs
was still the central tradition of the evolving discipline
of cycle analysis. Extrapolating from this tradition, they
argued that mismanaged financial conditions and high,
inflexible wage rates were combining to discourage investment, thus endowing a normal cyclical depression with

---

[13]Berle and Means, <u>Modern Corporation</u>, 355-357.

abnormal intensity.

Alvin Hansen of the University of Minnesota gave perhaps the fullest expression of this interpretative approach, with his book Economic Stabilization in an Unbalanced World of 1932. Hansen had established a reputation in the twenties as one of America's foremost students of business cycles.[14] In his book he brought to bear various emphases that were evolving out of neo-orthodox and cycle-oriented thought, both English and Continental. He dealt first with the financial-international disruptions caused by World War I and the unwise governmental policies undertaken in its aftermath. On top of wartime dislocation of trade patterns had been laid the disequilibrating burden of reparations payment.[15] Then, in his view, an even more dangerous imbalance was created by American preponderance after the war, and the contradictory policies we carried on. For purchase of American goods and for payment of war debts, we extended loans to Europe. But we made repayment of the loans virtually impossible by raising ever higher tariffs against European exports.

---

[14]He had written a major text, Business-Cycle Theory: Its Development and Present Status (Boston, 1927). This book probably still represents the best concise exposition of its subject as of the late 1920's.

[15]Alvin Hansen, Economic Stabilization in an Unbalanced World (New York, 1932), 1-64.

The diminution of our foreign lending after 1927 came not
only because of our involvement in stock speculation, but
because our policies had already enforced deflationary
tendencies abroad, which lowered demand for our loans.
Gold increasingly poured into America, accentuating price
disparities: Europe faced credit contraction and declining prices relative to America. In the end our policies
were pricing us out of foreign markets, our exports falling after 1928. Sheer illogical policy on our part,
especially tariff policy, had caused a grave distortion
of international equilibrium.[16]

Such were the conditions which, according to
Hansen, had played a primary role in aggravating an
ordinary depression. But Hansen took pains to describe
the ordinary course of the business cycle as wayward
enough. He cited with approval the ideas of Spiethoff
and other forerunners of Schumpeter in the Continental
investment-oriented school of cycle theory. Hansen
reiterated their view that great inventions and expansions
were themselves destabilizing forces, that progress was
inherently dynamic. He concluded that the present would
not be the last violent cyclical experience.[17]

---

[16]Ibid., 80-91, 112.

[17]Ibid., 309-309.

Yet Hansen further sought particular maladjustments which were exacerbating the cycle. He saw fit to discuss the rigidities which so involved writers in the institutionalist tradition. He agreed that disparities in price fall had deranged the price structure.[18] But Hansen saw with greater alarm the parallel rigidification of wage rates. Given his investment-based view of the cycle, the resistance of wages to a full decline seemed entirely to imperil normal economic revival. In this context Hansen railed at length against underconsumptionist as well as reflationist notions.[19]

The orthodox case against wrong-headed economic policies as responsible for the depth of the Depression was only hardened by the continuation of the Depression and the advent of the New Deal. In 1934 several economists of Harvard, under the leadership of Schumpeter, published a set of essays amounting to a virtual manifesto against the tendencies of New Era and New Deal policy. In the first essay, Schumpeter outlined the constructive necessity of periodic unimpeded depression. He urged that the only elements that had made for such an abnormally severe Depression were "non-economic." Not only the

---

[18]Ibid., 99-100.

[19]Ibid., 279, ff., 320-321, 365-366.

results of the war and reparations, but still worse:

> . . . impediments to the working of the gold
> standard, economic nationalism heaping mal-
> adjustment upon maladjustment, a fiscal policy
> incompatible with the smooth running of
> industry and trade, a mistaken wage policy,
> political pressure on the rate of interest,
> organized resistance to necessary adjustment
> and the like.[20]

In essentials Schumpeter's ideas paralleled Hansen's closely; only they were set forth more compactly and more shrilly. The foundations had been laid for Schumpeter's great work of 1942, Capitalism, Socialism, and Democracy, which would picture a transition to socialism forced by sheerly non-economic social influences.

An essay by Edward Chamberlin followed, on "Purchasing Power," which attacked all recent consumption-supporting notions. A greater testament to the inner logic of the orthodox position was hard to imagine: for Chamberlin had become by 1933 a world leader in the new school of "imperfect competition." This school had found variants of classical formal models of monopolistic price determination to apply to the current oligopolistic conditions in big industry at large.[21] The development of

---

[20]Douglass V. Brown et al., The Economics of the Recovery Program (New York, 1934), 15.

[21]Cf. Edward Chamberlin, The Theory of Monopolistic Competition (Cambridge, Mass., 1933); for discussion cf. Eric Roll, A History of Economic Thought (Englewood Cliffs, 1961), 470-479.

this school was the realization within the tradition of
equilibrium analysis of the general historical perspectives of Berle and Means' Modern Corporation. This was
a notable confluence which no doubt reinforced the critique
of rigid prices and their underconsumptionist effects.
Nonetheless, when it came to the interpretation of the
larger dynamics of the Depression, Chamberlin spoke
entirely without reference to his own preoccupations in the
field of microeconomic price mechanisms. He rather
directed his criticism at the high-wage policies of the
1920's and after! These he felt had tended to speed the
replacement of men with machines, to foster unemployment--
and to put upward pressure on prices.[22] The popular
obsession with purchasing power had obscured the simple
fact that investment had suffered far more in the
Depression, in terms of percentages, than consumption.
Finally, far too late, he asserted, more widespread
acknowledgement of the need to revive investment had
occurred, when the revival of 1933 had failed commensurately to rekindle investment.[23]

The statistics of the relative failure of investment were indeed increasingly stark. A study by Arthur

---

[22]Brown, et al., Economics of the Recovery, 35-37.

[23]Ibid., 30-31.

Tebbutt in 1933 showed that levels of physical consumption had held remarkably well in most essential goods, even through 1932. Tebbutt concluded, simply, that the New Deal had better reorient itself to the true problem--the heavier consumer durables, and, in particular, capital goods.[24] The English economist Lionel Robbins, in his influential The Great Depression, referred emphatically to Tebbutt's findings. Robbins employed them in the course of extending the orthodox interpretation towards a kind of over-consumptionism. He maintained that American policy, by holding wages and dividends high in the early Depression, had indeed buoyed consumption--but by the same token had so depleted the funds for investment as to strangle it. Not merely discouraged, adequate investment had been made literally impossible.[25]

Such then was the ferocity of the orthodox reaction to the New Era, and particularly to the new doctrines of high consumption. The left-wing orientation to consumption was viewed by the more orthodox writers as merely an amplification of the mistaken attitudes of the New Era. Liberals, for their part, dismissed the orthodox

[24]Arthur R. Tebbutt, "The Behavior of Consumption in Business Depression," Business Research Studies, No. 3, 1933, 20-21.

[25]Lionel Robbins, The Great Depression (London, 1934), 69-71.

approach as a new growth in a business-oriented rhetoric that had dominated the New Era.

Of course, the cluster of attitudes that had held sway in the late twenties had been loose enough, and over-confident enough so that such an angry, polarizing attack on them was, in the time of Collapse, a perfectly inevitable turn of events. Similarly, it was unlikely that writers such as Mitchell and Fisher, who had contributed so centrally to the New Optimism, would be able quickly to take an exciting initiative in the interpretation of its demise. And they did not. They did, however, interpret; and they at least succeeded in steering a humble course between the agitated extremes of the investment-consumption controversy.

Writing a brief article in 1933, Mitchell, with recantation where necessary, reworked his analysis of 1929. Now he descried heavy overspeculation in urban real estate and securities as key features in the boom and in the intensity of the Depression. The postwar imbalances in international trade and finance, he thought, had been a large aggravating burden. The weak condition of agriculture, and the generally steep fall of commodity prices, he adduced as more or less independent aspects of the Depression. Finally, the reduction in wage and profit distributions caused by the Depression, had in turn the effect of further intensifying it by lowering

consumption.[26] By working eclectically, Mitchell had
combined the financial-international factors stressed by
Hansen and the other investment-oriented analysis--with a
mild admixture of the underconsumptionist theme. The
effort was at once a sensible antidote to the more mono-
lithic explanations that were rampant, and a rather too
shaky synthesis to carry great conviction in those days of
cataclysm. Since Mitchell had not brought in the consump-
tion-related factors till late in the game, one might have
inferred that in truth the domestic and international
financial collapses had delivered the crucial initiating
blows of the deflationary spiral. In that case, Mitchell
had little to add to the accounts of the Depression that
were appearing daily in the newspapers. Still and all,
Mitchell had shown that the concept of "balance"--the New
Era's equal solicitude for investment and consumption--
might be revived. Yet strangely, balance seemed to have
become a formula pregnant with possibilities for a
cumulative downward interaction between investment and
consumption, rather than an emblem of their mutual
supportiveness under knowledgeable management.

There is no question that Mitchell was profoundly
alarmed over the future of the economic system. If his

[26]Mitchell, "Business Cycles," World Today
(Yearbook of the Encyclopedia Britannica), October 1933,
28.

interpretation seemed a confident enumeration of fortuitous
and temporary factors which had derailed stability, he elsewhere openly expressed more abiding fears. In his "Review
of Findings" in the large volume <u>Recent Social Trends in
the United States</u> compiled by a committee empowered by
Hoover, Mitchell wrote urgently and provocatively. He
broached problems of the broadest sort, such as that "our
capacity to produce goods changes faster than our capacity
to purchase":[27] He suggested that a vast effort was
required to bring "social invention" abreast of "mechanical invention."[28] He reiterated the concerns of Berle and
Means, that large business was gaining immense power, and
that its ownership was being shorn of control. Finally
he argued that it was likely that government would have to
arrogate large new functions in support of economic
balance.[29] His growing attraction to the formulations of
institutionalism, and even of all-out underconsumptionism,
had not indeed intruded into his interpretative analysis
<u>per se</u>. But interpretative controversy apparently seemed
far less important to him than social action to end the
Depression. He never did write at length on the interpretation of the Depression. If, when he did treat the

---

[27]Mitchell, "Review of Findings," in <u>Recent
Social Trends in the United States</u> (New York, 1934), xiii.

[28]<u>Ibid.</u>, xv.

[29]<u>Ibid.</u>, xxi-xxxiii.

latter, he held to a dispassionate and balanced approach,
he was all the time boldly readying himself to accept more
radical, reformist premises. After all, the role of
enlightened policy had been central to his 1929 characterization of economic balance. The Depression, whatever its
causes, seemed to demonstrate the need for a far more
powerful sort of policy. The continuity was fundamental
here, in Mitchell's progress. This continuity itself
probably contributed to what there was of theoretical
aloofness and ambiguity in his attitude. Such precisely,
in the end, was the mood of America as she travelled,
experimentally, from the New Era to the New Deal.

Irving Fisher, so highly identified with the New
Era, kept a somewhat similar detachment from the great
debate over consumption vs. investment. He emphasized,
almost exclusively, the role of domestic overindebtedness
in setting the stage for Collapse. Reversing his earlier
prediction that the stock market crash would not cause
deep deflation, Fisher conceded that stock market and
other speculation had indeed fatally raised the levels of
indebtedness. When liquidation came about in this
environment, a dangerous impulse was set in motion. The
race to liquidate debts brought about enough contraction
of currency and general deflation of prices to cause the
relative burden of remaining debts to grow. Hence the

liquidation was intensified; the process reinforced itself and would tend to carry on to the point of general bankruptcy. He added, however, that the original state of overexpansion of credit need not have led to catastrophe, had the Federal Reserve maintained a strongly stimulative policy of open-market purchases. For it seemed to him that the effects of the volume of money and credit on the movement of prices formed the most portentous economic nexus: if money contracted, prices fell, initiating general contraction _via_ profits and then production and employment.[30] Immediately after the Crash, Fisher had been more concerned about direct depressive effects on investment and consumption. Fisher's field of interest had always centered in monetary and price phenomena; but his increasingly concentrated focus on the dynamics of these elements seem to represent a stunned, almost evasive response to the fall of the vaunted New Era equilibrium.

In any case, Fisher's interpretative orientation to the financial sphere was parallel to Mitchell's, though Mitchell emphasized international aspects more and held a generally broader view. For both them prior speculative overextension (Fisher emphasizing the role of debt in this), and subsequent financial liquidation were the

---

[30]I. Fisher, "Debt-Deflation Theory of Great Depressions," _Econometrica_, v. 1, October 1933, 337-350.

central themes of the Depression. Both, too, instinctively reacted against deflation and had sought counter-
vailing action, supporting Hoover's policies of wage and
investment support from the outset. Ultimately, as dis-
equilibrium proved more devastating than they had imagined,
Mitchell worked hardest at preventing wage cuts and otherwise bolstering the consumption of the lower classes,
while Fisher concentrated on the elaboration of monetary
reflationist measures.[31] Both were eventually pushed to
moods highly tolerant of unorthodox intervention for
economic recovery.

Interpretatively, and in other ways, the views of
Mitchell and Fisher resembled those of John Maynard Keynes.
By 1930 Keynes' Treatise on Money had established him as a
leading exponent of the neo-orthodoxy, which in America
had fostered moderate New Era conception. The Treatise
argued bracingly that investment, and hence the business
cycle, could be regulated by central bank policy acting
through interest rates.[32] Keynes had, of course, much
earlier established a full-scale negative critique of
postwar economic policy and resultant imbalance. He had

[31]Cf. Joseph Dorfman, The Economic Mind in
American Civilization, v. 5 (New York, 1959), 667, 686.

[32]Keynes, A Treatise on Money (New York, 1930),
v. 2, 339-377.

characterized not only reparations and the terms of the
English return to gold, but also the high tariff policy
of America, as fraught with danger. Thus he set out
lines that Hansen and other economists would follow in
their interpretations of the Depression.[33] Keynes in the
Treatise further developed his interpretation of the
imbalance, emphasizing the high levels of postwar interest rates which had been the result of ravenous international demand for American loans (in turn the result of
the postwar imbalances favoring America). The high rate
of interest had, after the headiest part of the investment cycle was past, finally suffocated the drive to
invest.[34] Hence a single remedial policy could now have
restored relative health: central banks, Keynes felt,
must cooperate in driving down interest rates through
open-market purchases and other means.[35] As the
Depression worsened, Keynes expanded his description of
its pathology to include much more than interest rates;
he called for ever more strenuous reflationist policies,
ranging from maintenance of wages to vast government

---

[33]Keynes, _Essays in Persuasion_ (London, 1931), 3-73.

[34]Keynes, _Treatise_, v. 2, 378-381.

[35]_Ibid._, 385-387.

spending projects.[36] Yet his interpretation retained its
English, internationalist perspective. In essence, he
viewed the spreading breakdown and the lack of enlightened
governmental policies together, as a chain of frightened
responses fostered by the international gold standard--a
virtual "competitive campaign of deflation."[37] This
absurd spiral of deflation tending toward universal
bankruptcy was rather like the one Fisher described in
1933, except that Keynes usually construed it in international terms. But Keynes also dealt with the specific
evils of panicky debt-liquidation, urging that the bankers
of the world, by trying to save themselves individually,
were collectively "bent on suicide."[38]

All in all, while Keynes' response to the
Depression was quicker, and bolder in terms of policy,
than those of Mitchell and Fisher, his interpretative
reflex was similar. His emphasis, including his early
focus on interest rates, was on the ramifying effects of
financial conditions and mechanisms. His views were,
of course, more internationalist than Mitchell's or
Fisher's. Not only his international emphasis grew from

[36]Cf. Keynes, "Saving and Spending" (January
1931), Essays in Persuasion, 148-167.

[37]Ibid., "The End of the Gold Standard" (September
1931), 293.

[38]Ibid., "The Consequences to the Banks of the
Collapse of Money Values"(August 1931), 178, 168-177.

English conditions. His extraordinary prescience and
promptness in developing his critique and remedies, surely
related to his location in England--where depression marred
the entire postwar scene. In any case, his interpretative
approach, for all the trenchancy of its attack on conven-
tion, evidenced the same hesitancy that was found in the
writings of the old New Era authorities of America.
Hesitancy to find anything basically wrong in investment
per se, consumption per se, or in the relations between
them: this was associated with the chiefly financial
interpretation, no less for Keynes than for the Americans.[39]

The groups which we have designated orthodox and
neo-orthodox comprised the bulk of the recognized
economics profession, and were certainly not divided in
all matters. The financial elements of the Depression
figured largely in all of their interpretations. But a
great difference was made by the refusal of the neo-
orthodoxy (at least of Mitchell and Keynes) to see the
financial crisis and the Depression as strictly working
through the sphere of investment. In opposing wage cuts,

---

[39]On Keynes in the early thirties, see Lawrence
Klein, The Keynesian Revolution (New York, 1949), 1-30.
Klein's description is not out of accord with ours;
except that he, oddly, refers to Keynes as a "classical"
economist in the period of the Treatise. One would
think that Keynes' dedication to money-management
warrants the prefix "neo-."

they were holding to the New Era notion of consumption as
a factor of independent force in general activity. While
not clarifying their revision of Say's Law, they were
maintaining distance from its dogmatic orientation toward
investment as the prime and sufficient mover of economic
conditions. In the General Theory, Keynes would in a
sense return to the investment centered tradition. But
that would be to remold it from within, emphasizing the
inherent instability of investment. For now, the neo-
orthodoxy of economic management held a gently exploratory
position, with virtually indeterminate theoretical foundations.

Surely this evolved New Era approach, while not
fully explaining itself, was increasingly conceiving
economic equilibrium as unstable, frangible, dynamic.
That financial crisis could bring a cumulative downswing
of investment and consumption without end, suggested a
new inability in the economy to weather storms, a new
proclivity to magnify then into hurricanes. The newly
disruptive factors were loudly proclaimed by the unorthodox to consist in tendencies to underconsumption, by the
orthodox to reside in impediments to investment. The New
Era neo-orthodoxy, at least in America, had already helped
oversee a regime which, to the best of their understanding,
had notably emancipated both investment and consumption.
Hence they were unable to see logic in critiques biased

toward either sphere. They concluded rather naturally
that both arms of economic policy would have to be
strengthened, either directly or through monetary refla-
tion.

Oddly, while immersing themselves in questions of
current policy, thinkers of the chastened New Era type
helped set the stage for a freeing of interpretation from
obsession with previous policy. Such obsession embodied
the greatest common ground between the polarized schools
of criticism of New Era imbalances. The orthodox critique
was unified, as much as by its orientation to investment,
by its attack on misguided policy--tariff, high-wage, and
anti-deflationary policies. Liberals in turn inveighed
against high-price, low-wage, and to a lesser degree those
same international policies.[40] It was the heyday of
institutionalist criticism. But this heyday saw the dissi-
pation of what little sense of unity had evolved in the
institution-centered approach over thirty tortuous years.
The neo-orthodoxy was unconsciously turning away from
institutionalist analysis, and searching for more
strictly cyclical modes. Writers who had helped make

---

[40]Arthur Adams, an influential and prolific underconsumptionist cycle theorist, fully incorporated American
tariff and lending policies into his view of the crisis:
they had artificially raised consumption just as had
installment buying. Cf. The Trend of Business, 1922-32
(New York, 1932), 15, 24.

policy for the New Era (though they now conceded that financial arrangements had been very lax), were inclined to recast their entire notion of the economy in more dynamic terms, rather than merely to reevaluate past economic management.

New dynamic and autonomous modes of movement in the economy, irresistible by mere manipulations of policy (at least on the modest scale of policy in the 1920's): such were in fact to be the major lines of inquiry in economic thought and interpretation. As we shall see, tendencies toward such reconstruction were already bearing fruit by 1932-34. Eventually Keynes, Hansen, and Schumpeter were all to enter, in the mid-thirties, grand phases of reorientation to dynamic problems. But first the contribution of J. M. Clark was to come to maturity. It would represent an evolution of the most dynamic ideas of the 1920's, filling the void in neo-orthodox conception, and mediating in the contention of pro-investment and pro-consumption schools.

These latter groups had carried institutionally oriented criticism, in either direction, so far as to undermine it. Later, as the focus of economic controversy gravitated toward more autonomous or deterministic schemata, the opposing wings of the institution-centered method would tend to coalesce. The result would be a combined

critique of price and wage rigidity, with little relation
to underconsumption: in fact, this school would best
embody the traditional orthodox hankering after classically
competitive laissez-faire.[41] This, in turn, would expose
the truth that the fundamental method of liberal academic
institutionalism (the critique of rigid prices) had represented a largely negative thrust against the body of neo-
classical doctrine. Positive thrusts would have to come
fairly strictly from the formulations of rounded, longer-
term dynamic analysis, i.e. business cycle theory. These
things would not be clear to the economics profession at
large until the thirties had passed: but both of the
relatively static disciplines of the neo-orthodox synthesis of the 1920's--equilibrium theory, and institutionalist
tradition--had been deeply debilitated by the pace of
events from 1929 to 1933.

The theoretical objective of America's distinctive
institutionalist economics had always been the construction
of a truly historical or evolutionary alternative to
classical formalism. The magnitude of this task was now
first felt, as the Depression destroyed the assumptions of
equilibrium economics--and hence rendered institutionalism's
arsenal of critical weaponry obsolete. As the orthodox

----

[41]See below, pp. 109, 138-150.

equilibrium orientation finally became a primarily critical discipline, absorbing institutionalist analysis of
rigidities, and inverting its former descriptions of
economic reality, institutionalism was, simply, usurped.
Viewing the situation most abstractly for a moment further,
one must conclude that institutionalism, if it were to
continue to embody the pragmatic and relevant way of
seeing, faced a terrible challenge. It must become what
it had not meant to be: institutionalism must become a
cycle theory, by the sheer force of its inquiring spirit.
Fortunately, in concrete historical terms, the early
career of J. M. Clark, and other writers, had made such a
transition possible. But that does not change the
momentousness of the abstract turning point that obtained
for social perception in America.

CHAPTER III

CLARK, AND IDEAS OF AUTONOMOUS CAUSES

OF THE BREAKDOWN

By 1934 several lines of approach had been laid
out which dealt with the Collapse without reference to the
issues of institutional reflex and policy, which had so
engrossed the New Era and the reaction to it. To a large
extent these approaches would seek to explain what had
been newly dangerous in the economy of the 1920's without
denying that it had possessed a new exhiliration. The
tendencies in New Era thought to conceive a heightened
momentum of technological innovation, and a newly powerful
inter-reaction between investment and consumption, need
not be contradicted. It merely had to be shown that, far
from being cultivated and controlled by society, these
stimuli were running a course that led to momentous
reversal. This impression could be conveyed in various
ways, each of which assumed a new and fundamental volatility in the relations of investment and consumption.
Certain interpretors held that the great new markets for
consumer goods--such as autos--had become, in one sense or

another, "saturated," creating a sudden dearth of outlets
for investment. Others saw a new potential for deflation
in the very nature of the consumer durable goods: their
durability implied postponability of their replacement,
and the possibility of intensification of an ordinary
depression by such postponement. Finally, J. M. Clark's
concept of the potential "accelerator" interaction between
investment and consumption gained new recognition. The
"accelerator" had been known to cycle theorists in the
1920's; now it would come to have a more haunting effect.
Clark's work of 1934, Strategic Factors in Business Cycles,
reasserted the accelerator principle and related it to
other influences which had fostered the dynamic extremes
of the cycle of 1921-33.

The uniqueness and power of Clark's intellectual
contribution, from the second to the fourth decades of the
century, are hard to overestimate. It has been mentioned
that Clark strove in the twenties to render "dynamic" the
conceptions of economic analysis. It remains to describe
the extent to which he achieved this goal, particularly in
his formulation of the accelerator principle. Son of
John Bates Clark, one of the greatest American expositors
of neo-classical static analysis, Clark did his graduate
work at Columbia. He taught economics from 1908, notably
at the University of Chicago from 1915 to 1926, when he
took up his retired father's position as professor of

economics at Columbia. Clark's seminal contribution was
made as early as 1917 in an article setting forth the
workings of the concept of acceleration. His point of
departure was Wesley Mitchell's work, Business Cycles, of
1913. There Mitchell had demonstrated that the fluctuations in production of industrial equipment were more
marked than the fluctuations of other indexes in the business cycle. Clark fashioned a highly suggestive interpretation of this fact.[1] The basic principle of this interpretation was that demand for the means of production
varies "not with the volume of the demand for the finished
product, but rather with the acceleration of that demand."[2]
Starting at a slack or depressed period, thus, a relatively slight increase in demand for a given finished
product would bring about a much larger percentage gain
in the demand for equipment for the production of that

---

[1]J. M. Clark, "Business Acceleration and the Law
of Demand: A Technical Factor in Economic Cycles,"
reprinted in Readings in Business Cycle Theory,
American Economic Association (Philadelphia, 1944), 235-
257.
    The line of argument Clark followed was, roughly,
precedented, particularly in the work of 1909-1913 by
the French cycle theorist, Albert Aftalion. Still,
Clark appears to have developed the approach essentially
on his own. More importantly, accelerator theory came
to the attention of other economists in the 1920's and
1930's chiefly through the work of Clark. (For the
thought of Aftalion, and other backgrounds, as well as
full discussion of the accelerator, see Hansen, Business
Cycles (1964), 347-393.)

[2]Clark, "Business Acceleration," 253.

product. This accounted for the steep rise in investment goods which appeared to initiate the prosperous phase of the cycle. Similarly, at the turning point in the cycle (from prosperity to depression), a mere slowing of the rate of expansion of demand for the final product could cause an absolute decline in the demand for means of production. Though statistically investment reached its peak prior to consumption, the former could be seen as following the latter after all. For mere trends in consumption produced, in Clark's view, intensified movements in--and even reversals of--investment.[3]

Clark restated his description of the place of acceleration in the cycle, in his large work of 1923 on The Economics of Overhead Costs. Actually Clark was less concerned there with the business cycle per se, than with its social costs. He developed the concept of "overhead" into a broad tool of social accounting. Not only all forms of productive plant and equipment, but also the entire labor force, he argued, must be viewed as embodying ongoing "overhead" charges upon economic society.[4] In this context he pointed out the absurdity of the

---

[3]Ibid., passim.

[4]Clark, Studies in the Economics of Overhead Costs (Chicago, 1923), 357-385ff.

behavior of individual firms in cyclical or other depressions. Firms attempted to protect their own fixed capital
by firing labor, or by cancelling purchases from other
firms: hence they merely caused the disuse of others'
overhead equipment and the social overhead of labor. It
was in this frankly philosophical context that Clark con-
ducted his search for purely technical factors making for
cyclical instability. Such was the breadth and calm of
his intellect. His notion of social overhead had the
uncompromising logic and morality necessary to a humane
treatment of the problems of industrial society. His
description of the accelerator principle, on the other
hand, entailed a use of induction and complex abstraction
in the manner of the physical scientist.

Nor were Clark's concerns lacking in connective
development. His broader focus on the concept of overhead
easily harmonized with his specific treatment of the business cycle. The accelerator was a way of demonstrating the
extreme fitfulness of business' method of constructing its
overhead. The accelerator-caused cyclical downturn could
be seen as a secondary effect of the testy reluctance of
business to add to overhead costs, whenever the slightest
doubt as to the future of the market could be raised.
Moreover, these constructions led Clark quite directly to
the conclusion that the cycle could be overcome by

government policies of a concentrated sort. Since he saw
the accelerator-induced depression as rooted in a wrong-
headed and myopic concept of overhead costs on the part
of business, Clark was forthright in suggesting investment in public works and unemployment insurance to combat
depression. These policies would bolster the more vulner-
able areas of the general social overhead.[5]

The coherence of Clark's analysis of the overhead
element in prices has often drawn praise from commentators.
Clark has been seen as perhaps the most successful mediator
between classical price-oriented economics and the perspectives of critical institutionalism.[6] The institutionalist strain in Clark was even more fully manifested than
before in his book Social Control of Business of 1926.
There he described the evolution of industry out of the
classical conditions of small competitive units and into
the modern system of large business. In urging the exercise of social control, he employed the characteristic
institutionalist critique of monopolistic tendencies in
business.[7] But the essay of 1927 we have mentioned

---

[5]Clark, ibid., 407-15.

[6]Cf. Dorfman, Economic Mind, v. 5, 458, 461;
Gruchy, Modern Economic Thought, 401.

[7]J. M. Clark, Social Control of Business
(Chicago, 1926).

above, showed that Clark did not leave behind his concern
with the special challenge of the business cycle.[8] We
have said that the most fruitful area of synthesis between
equilibrium economics and institutionalism lay in the
field of cycle analysis, or dynamic economics. And
Clark's accelerator-cycle embodied the most dynamic of
the contemporary formulations of the cycle. Even apart
from the context of Clark's investigation of the dual
nature of overhead costs, accelerator theory suggested
synthetic possibilities in cycle analysis which might
modify the entire historical debate between neo-classical
and institutionalist economics.

For if Clark's accelerator formulation were true,
he would have discovered precisely the sort of blind
"culumative" cyclical principle that he had sought to
replace the neo-classical self-limiting mechanisms. Also,
in comparison to the accelerator concept, the neo-
institutionalist works of the 1930's typified by that of
Berle and Means, seemed unforgivably tepid and static.
More importantly for the specific interpretation of the
Great Depression, Clark's methodology seemed to promise
mediation between the more orthodox investment-oriented
approaches and the strict underconsumptionism that was

---

[8]On the essay on dynamics, see above, pp. 31-32.

gaining sway in institutionalist and radical conception.

Clark most forcefully pictured the kind of dynamic interaction between consumption and investment which
might be at play in the business cycle, in a section of
the Economics of Overhead Costs. First he stated the
initial influence of the accelerator in the cycle--that
an increase of one dollar in the demand for consumer's
goods produces ". . . in time, an increase of two dollars
in the output of equipment. . . ."[9] Then Clark added
that ordinarily "most of this two dollars is spent for
consumable goods" and hence reacts back again on the
finished goods industries. This mutual stimulation might
go on until the capital goods makers simply cannot expand
further, hence do not contribute to the increase of consumption, and therefore set in motion the accelerator
diminution of investment.[10] Here Clark's notion of the
cumulative momentum of the process anticipated in a
large sense the Kahn-Keynes investment-multiplier.[11]
Clark's sketch, of course, still relied on the accelerator effect of consumption on investment to foster the
strategic increments of income. In any case, it is

---

[9]Clark, Overhead Costs, 393.

[10]Ibid., 393-394.

[11]On the Keynesian multiplier, see below, p. 118.

clear that Clark was thinking in terms of an elementary
income-multiplier.[12] His work was already providing a
basis for the most dynamic formulations of post-
Keynesian business cycle theory, i.e., the "accelerator-
multiplier" model.[13]

Clark's work on the accelerator--in fact his
early work of 1917--achieved recognition by Wesley
Mitchell. In his most tersely lucid piece on the business
cycle, an article of 1923, Mitchell mentioned Clark and
the accelerator principle. He used it as one element in
his discussion of the several factors that together
caused the turning point from prosperity to depression.
He more fully emphasized the role of overextension of
credit, high bond and other interest rates, generally
rising prices and costs, and the development of profit
weakness in the less successful industries.[14] In the
context of these various deterrents to continued increase
in investment, Mitchell allowed a potential role for the
accelerator effect. Mitchell took care to describe the

---

[12]Clark arrived more precisely at a concept of
the investment multiplier in 1931-35; cf. Dorfman,
Economic Mind, v. 5, 762-764. See also, below, p. 94,
note 49.

[13]See below, pp. 124, 193 ff.

[14]This essay was Mitchell's introduction to the
National Bureau's Report on Business Cycles and Unemploy-
ment, 1923, reprinted in Business Cycle Theory, American
Economic Association (1944), 43-60.

cycle as involving elements which might vary historically, producing more or less extreme cycles. Nor did he seem to consider the accelerator as peculiarly linked to the problems of the sharper cyclical movements. The accelerator passed into the growing tradition of cycle analysis, then, without much excitement. Its workings were again described as a possible aspect of the cycle in the most important general works on the cycle in the late twenties in America, by Mitchell and Alvin Hansen.[15] But these theorists made no further mention of the accelerator principle in their interpretative writings on the Depression in the early thirties.

The accelerator theory stood as a kind of extreme, highly abstract symbol of the tendencies of economic thought in the 1920's toward focus on the dynamic interplay between consumption and investment. Never before had the importance of a rising consumption been so widely felt. Perhaps Clark's work on the accelerator helped to stimulate the concern of economists over consumption. But in any case, the conviction spread that the problem of consumption was well in hand, particularly due to the successes of the doctrine of high wages. As we have

---

[15]Mitchell, Business Cycles--The Problem and Its Setting (New York, 1927), 44; Hansen, Business-Cycle Theory (Boston, 1927), 112-114. By 1927 Mitchell seemed to have less interest in the accelerator formulation than in 1923. Hansen's book of 1927 gave a rather more serious treatment of the accelerator than did Mitchell's.

seen, men as different as Tugwell and Mitchell seemed reassured on that score by the late twenties. Yet this ought not to have fully allayed fears, if one looked at matters in the light of the accelerator concept. For, again, the latter raised the possibility of cumulative economic depression resulting from a mere slowing in the rate of growth of consumption. Ultimately, the accelerator principle conferred a primacy upon movements in consumption which perhaps had more in common with the notions of frank underconsumptionists like Foster and Catchings than with the balanced constructions of a Mitchell.

If an accelerator-based interpretation of the Collapse were to be developed, a fuller explanation was needed of the primacy, the leading role, of consumption in the 1920's. A potential explanation was suggested by the obvious fact of the dominance of consumer durables-- such as autos, housing, refrigerators, radios--in the economy of the twenties. The growing orientation of the economy to the markets for these finished, often costly, and inessential consumer goods was making an impression on economic observers. Foster and Catchings, in the context of their account of the dangers of underconsumption, had given the credit for the high prosperity of the twenties to the irreplaceable stimulus of the automobile industry. They described the vital stimulus afforded by capital investment in auto factories; and they sometimes urged that demand for autos must continue to grow (not merely stablize at high levels), or such investment would fall off.[16] They also considered that installment purchases of autos had importantly boosted that industry. But here again they speculated that installment sales would have to increase continually in order to sustain their initial stimulating effects.[17] They used such arguments as adjuncts to their basic notions on the tendencies toward simple underconsumption and the need for more powerful artificial support for consumption. As may be readily seen, some of their methodology closely paralleled that of accelerator theory. Further, their emphasis on the automobile provided a concrete basis for the orientation of their economics to consumption.

Undoubtedly the rise of the great new consumer goods such as autos underlay much of the general concern over consumption which economists felt in the 1920's. When they expressed doubts as to its adequate continuance, they often referred to potential "saturation" of a given

---

[16]Foster and Catchings, Business Without a Buyer (Boston, 1927), 77-90.

[17]Ibid., 57-76.

consumer market. As was mentioned above, Irving Fisher in 1930 did consider it possible that "saturation" had been reached in the markets for housing and autos.[18] This notion seemed ominous enough: it suggested that the outlook for consumption in these areas might be so bleak as to discourage investment in them. In other words, saturation might be seen as a condition which ushered in a sharp downward accelerator effect. Yet Fisher never developed these matters, instead turning to his financial, "debt-deflation" interpretation of the Depression. It seemed difficult for the New Era mind to contemplate at length the possibility that the marvelous expansion of consumers goods had come so quickly to a true saturation point. Fisher seemed to share the attitude of Hoover and the others who had written the introduction to the National Bureau Report of 1929. There a passing concession had been made that, someday in the future, there might be reached certain "remote saturation points."[19] The concept was not discussed there, any more than by Fisher. It seemed to speak for itself to the consumer-oriented New Era, and yet not really to inspire the concern that it might have.

---

[18]Cf. above, p. 27.

[19]National Bureau Report on Recent Economic Changes (New York, 1929), xix.

In the early Depression the concept of market
saturation did not receive the development it seemed to
warrant. Like the accelerator principle, it suggested
an interpretative middle course--but was overshadowed by
the polemical constructions of the stricter underconsumptionists and the financial-investment schools of
thought. Saturation, particularly in the auto market,
perhaps found fullest discussion in the works of Stuart
Chase. Chase had been in the twenties a leading
popularizer of Veblenite views and an exposer of frauds
against the consumer. In the Depression Chase moved
quickly to an underconsumptionist position, claiming that
industry was in a state of overcapacity even for "Utopian"
levels of consumption.[20] But he sometimes stressed the
more limited point that the auto had been basic to
prosperity, and had arrived at market-saturation by 1929.[21]
In his portentously titled A New Deal (1932), Chase
mustered an imposing list of causes of the Depression,
ranging from international imbalance to over-use of
installment credit. Underconsumptionist themes still
predominated in his gallantly eclectic treatment. But
now he described the problem of autos more specifically.

---

[20]Stuart Chase, The Nemesis of American Business
and Other Essays (New York, 1931), 79.

[21]Ibid., 169-171.

He asserted that real expansion in the auto industry had
come to an end as demand had been met, leaving finally a
mere "replacement market" for autos. It was not a
matter of total saturation, but of an end to the need for
investment in increasing capacity.[22] Concluding on the
dire straits of the economy in general, Chase held both
that consumption was too restricted, and that outlets for
investment were largely "saturated." Hence normal
recovery seemed precluded all round.[23]

Chase, in his rough and undeveloped way, had
taken an important step. He speculated, forshadowing the
Keynes-Hansen school of investment stagnation, that
besides the old, saturated investment outlets, there
simply were not new ones large enough to buoy prosperity.
These bold assumptions, embracing the conditions of consumption and of investment, yielded as fundamentally
black a picture as one could draw. Interestingly, these
assumptions were implied, in a subtle way, by the
accelerator concept of depression. Its logic was based
on an idea of the effect of demand patterns upon extant
industries. That is, it assumed that sudden new forms of
investment would not appear late in the cycle to counter

---

[22]Chase, A New Deal (New York, 1932). 130.

[23]Ibid., 131-132.

overall slowdown in the growth of consumption. As to
saturation, that need not advance far at all to bring
the accelerator into operation. Even if Chase had over-
stated the degree of saturation of demand for autos and
other consumers goods, he had described a situation in
which the accelerator might do damage. In any case,
while working with cruder notions than the accelerator,
Chase had made an approach to the essential method of
the latter: the interplay between investment and consumption. And, more or less in the vein of parts of the
1920's work of Foster and Catchings, he had discussed
concrete problems, that of autos in particular.

Chase's sort of heterodox interpretation
received a form of higher sanction in a campaign address
of Franklin Roosevelt, given at the Commonwealth Club of
San Francisco in September, 1932. Much of the speech
was unique in Roosevelt's campaign, and designed for the
Progressive and Bull Moose atmosphere of California
politics.[24] The interpretative outlook of the address
was based on a plaintive underconsumptionism. Its assertions that "our economic plant is built," and that the

[24]Cf. Frank Freidel, Franklin D. Roosevelt:
The Triumph (Boston, 1956), 353. For the text of the
speech, cf. Samuel Rosenman, ed., The Public Papers and
Addresses of Franklin D. Roosevelt, v. 1 (New York,
1938), 742-756.

task at hand was distribution, "meeting the problem of underconsumption," were stark and unqualified. The assumption that the age of industry-building was at an end clearly broached the question of dearth of investment outlets, although this theme was not developed. The Commonwealth Club address has been considered by Schlesinger to have "caught up poignantly the intellectual moods of the early Depression."[25] This was most obvious in the anti-big-business passages of the speech; these were typical of Adolf Berle, who had conceived it in outline for Roosevelt. But in truth some of the implications of the speech for economic history were more alarming than Chase's ideas, or even the later Keynesian notions of stagnation in a "mature economy"--and certainly were rare in Berle's writing of the time.[26] All in all, the San Francisco speech contained brief, but highly suggestive extrapolations from the underconsumptionist concern over various forms of "saturation."[27]

---

[25]Arthur Schlesinger, Jr., Crisis of the Old Order (Boston, 1957), 425.

[26]For a more usual expression of Berle's ideas, cf. Adolf A. Berle, "A High Road for Business," Scribner's Magazine, v. 93, June, 1933, 325-332. Here Berle speaks both of business "irresponsibility" and of general "overabundance"; but the idea of the end of the age of investment is not directly implied.

[27]Though approaches to the idea of a "mature" economy, in which expansion was threatened, were

The attunement of the economy of the 1920's to
the demand for consumer durables was found by commentators to entail other dangers besides simple saturation.
In fact, the rising proportion of durable products per se,
including machinery and other investment goods, was discussed as bringing on new instability. The fullest articulation of this idea appeared in the work of Frederick
C. Mills of 1932, Economic Tendencies in the United
States. Mills had been an important researcher for the
National Bureau after 1924, and a professor of economics
and statistics at Columbia from 1931. Mills' book,
written under the auspices of the National Bureau, was a
monumental general and statistical study of the economy
in the prewar and postwar periods. More unified than
the series of monographs that had made up the National
Bureau Report of 1929, the Mills study quickly became the
closest thing to a general authority on the economy.
Part of its authority stemmed from its depression-
oriented concluding portions. These, however, were
cautiously exploratory and represented several strands of
interpretative attitude. Speaking most broadly about the

---

extremely rare, Roosevelt's speech was not entirely
unique in the early 1930's. A perhaps more direct
statement of the mature economy theme was made, interestingly, by Felix Frankfurter, in an article, "Social
Issues Before the Supreme Court," Yale Review, v. 22
March, 1933, 475-496.

twenties, Mills described a situation of intense technological and organizational change--nonetheless containing
"elements of structural rigidity and inflexibility which
were apparently growing in strength."[28] Price rigidity
in particular, due to monopolistic and semi-monopolistic
influences, seemed the major impediment to smooth evolution.[29] Thus Mills incorporated the great theme of
institutionalist criticism, virtually superimposing it
upon the recent conceptions of the New Era.

Mills' discussion of the problem of durable goods
was partly joined to his critique of price rigidity, and
partly a large theme in its own right. Most broadly,
Mills characterized the increasing orientation of the
economy toward goods for which demand was highly elastic,
as entailing a new instability. These goods of elastic
demand included inessential or luxury products and durable
goods. This entire range of products seemed inherently
subject to market fluctuation more than were staple goods
such as food and clothing. Durable goods included the
most rapidly multiplying products of the 1920's, from
machinery and other capital goods to housing, autos, and
the other great consumer goods. Mills computed that

---

[28]Frederick C. Mills, Economic Tendencies in the
United States (New York, 1932), 533.

[29]Ibid., 557.

durable goods had grown at a rate of 5.9% per annum from
1922 to 1929, while non-durable goods had grown at a rate
of only 2.8%. Durable goods had comprised roughly 26% of
all production in the prewar period; by the twenties the
figure was already about 34%.[30] An element which had contributed to price rigidity, Mills held, was the rising
output of durable capital goods. Following the views
most publicized by Clark, Mills asserted that this trend
resulted in higher fixed or overhead costs, and hence in
more rigid industrial prices.[31] Yet, though Mills did
not say so, the more general index of durable goods
which he discussed seemed a more concentrated chronicle
of potential instability than those limited aspects of it
which might have made for price rigidity. In any case,
the two arguments had separate force. The treatment of
price rigidity stood firmly in the institutionalist tradition, as developed by Clark, Tugwell, Means. Mills
himself would later expand his own contribution to this
school, with his massive documentation of price movements
in the Depression.[32] Meanwhile, in his discussion of the
durable goods factor, he had set forth a problem entirely

---

[30]Ibid., 533-534.

[31]Ibid., 557.

[32]See below, pp. 145-150.

independent of the critique of monopolistic price policy.
The overall problem of durable goods suggested a purely
"technical" approach rather like the accelerator principle of Clark, and perhaps complementary to it. Mills,
very like Clark, was working for a synthesis of the
institutionalist approach with conceptions of a more
strictly dynamic, cycle-oriented nature.

The matter of the elastic demand for durable
goods was receiving occasional notice elsewhere in the
early Depression. Alvin Hansen, in the course of his
largely orthodox work of 1932 described above, made
mention of this question. In one place, while restating
his larger concern with the failure of wages to fall
sufficiently to encourage investment, Hansen speculated
that another possible cause for the unprecedented severity
of the Depression might lie in the new role of durables.
Since capital goods were the most highly fluctuating
element of economic activity, the increased use of fixed
capital perhaps implied a secular trend toward cyclical
movements of greater amplitude. He mentioned too that
the rising proportion of luxury goods of elastic demand
probably added to instability.[33] Similar passing mention
of this complex of factors was made by Stuart Chase. In

_____

[33]Hansen, _Economic Stabilization in an Unbalanced
World_ (New York, 1932), 365-366.

A New Deal, Chase mentioned that demand for luxury goods
was hardest hit by the stock market crash, and by the
Depression in general.[34] Whether a writer's orientation
was to investment, as with Hansen, or to consumption, as
with Chase, the new dynamic possibilities related to the
very products of the economy of the 1920's might find a
place in his interpretation.

More pointed treatment of these problems was
given in articles of 1932 and 1934 by Malcolm Rorty.
Rorty, who had been a chief organizer of the National
Bureau of Economic Research, and an executive of leading
telephone and telegraph companies, made an engaging case.
Arguing against the glib overinvestment-underconsumption-
ist interpretation, Rorty held that only in agriculture
had any essential condition of overproduction been
reached in the 1920's. If industry had overcapacity,
this was perfectly normal: industry ordinarily worked
at 70-80% of capacity. The true problem, Rorty
succinctly summarized as a new "sensitivity," due to

. . . increasing efficiency and the correspond-
ing devotion of a greater proportion of our
energies to the production of luxuries and of
capital and other durable goods, the consumption
of which may be drastically curtailed in times
of crises.[35]

[34]Chase, New Deal, 127.

[35]Malcolm C. Rorty, "The Equation of Economic
Balance," Harvard Business Review, v. 7, April 1934, 282-
283.

Hence a normal cyclical downturn was intensified, bringing on a state of "apparent surpluses of industrial
equipment, housing, etc." which in turn acted as great
barriers to recovery.[36]

Clearly Rorty gave the factor of durability a
more central place in his interpretation of the Depression than any other observer. He had stressed it since
1932, and may well have directly influenced Mills, during
discussions sponsored by the Bureau in which both men
took part. In any case, J. M. Clark also attended the
discussions, and there absorbed the Rorty-Mills attitude
toward durable goods.[37] This viewpoint formed a major
theme in Clark's work Strategic Factors in Business
Cycles, published in 1934.[38] Clark had been asked to
join the discussions among the economists who were
compiling statistical studies for the Bureau and to employ
this exposure in the writing of a more theoretical work
on the problems of cyclical instability.[39] Clark's

---

[36]Ibid., 283.

[37]On the discussions, cf. J. M. Clark,
Strategic Factors in Business Cycles (New York, 1934),
ix, Introduction by the Committee on Recent Economic
Changes.

[38]Clark mentioned his general debt to Mills, but
seemed to connect the emphasis on durables with Rorty, cit-
ing Rorty's early article, "How May Business Revival Be
Forced?" Harvard Business Review Supp., v. 10, April 1932,
385-398. Clark, Strategic Factors, 97, 109.

[39]Ibid., 27-36; Introduction, ix-xi.

book was sponsored by the Committee on Recent Economic Changes, which remained the ultimate authority behind the great studies of the Bureau. That the Committee, a bureaucratic remnant of the Hooverian age (it still included Young and Raskob), chose Clark for this unique task, was evidence of both acumen and fortitude on its part. A kind of official imprimatur was being given to an ever more dynamic approach. Mills' work represented a stride in this direction; and now Clark's Strategic Factors carried the Mills-Rorty notions into synthesis with dynamic accelerator method.

In a general sense, Clark's combined approach to the role of overhead costs and to accelerator effects had laid the basis for the Mills-Rorty concept of elastic demand for durables. For Clark, the 1934 work was a very straightforward development out of his earlier views, easily incorporating the problem of consumer durables. In fact, Clark merely rephrased his description of the accelerator principle, tying it directly to durable goods in general, as follows: he spoke of

> . . . the general principle of intensified fluctu-
> ations of derived demand for durable goods. That
> is, the demand for new supplies of durable goods
> fluctuates more intensely than demand for the
> current services these goods render.[40]

---

[40]Ibid., 33.

Clark went on to discuss housing and autos in this context. His point was to view the total stock of such
goods in the possession of consumers as a quantity
precisely parallel to the total stock of producers goods
or overhead capital. The "current services" of consumer
durables (say, the use of an auto for a year), or of
durable capital (say, the use of a machine for a year) had
in common that they exhausted only a small part of the
total life and worth of the durable good. In either
case, small net increments in demand for the "current
services" could lead to large gains in expenditure on
the production of the durables which rendered the
services. By the same token, the heart of the accelerator principle Clark saw to hold for consumers durables:
if the rate of growth in demand for the current services
decreased, an absolute decline in production of the
durables might result. Then too, if demand for the
current services failed to grow, and the total stock
remained unchanged, with demand for replacements of used
up portions of the total stock holding steady--production
would undergo a very large absolute decline.[41]

Having formally applied accelerator theory to the
category of consumer durables, Clark went on to describe

---

[41]Ibid., 27-33.

further the instability that might be connected with
them. Here his discussion was similar to the views of
Mills and Rorty. Clark pointed to the possibility that
during depression purchases for replacement of older
consumer durables might be postponed, thus greatly curtailing current production. Clark carefully related
this possibility to his previous description of the
accelerator, treating it as an extension of the latter
effect. The accelerator provided for large fluctuation
in the output of durables: replacement trends merely
accentuated fluctuation further.[42] Clark gave a concrete
example of the extremity of the movements that followed
so naturally from the conditions he had described. He
referred to the statistics on automobile registration
and production: a mere 9% decrease in registrations had
brought about a 75% decrease in production from 1929 to
1932.[43] The withholding of net new purchases and of
replacement purchases as well had brought the auto
industry nearly to a halt, with no great diminution in
the use of autos. Such were the effects that Mills, and
especially Rorty, had feared. But only in the context of
Clark's accelerator method did they begin to have full,
and awesome, comprehensibility.

---

[42]Ibid., 36-37.

[43]Ibid., 36.

91

Clark also characterized in bold terms the addi-
tional instability lent to consumer durables by their
purchase on installment credit. Clark reiterated that
his point had been to show production of durables as
subject to sharp fluctuations irrespective of the movement of general levels of income. The use of credit for
the purchase of durables heightened still further these
fluctuations. Clark concluded pointedly on the entire
matter: since durable goods, often bought on credit,
were increasingly important in the economy,

> . . . it may well be that, if no effective means
> of stabilization are found, business cycles in
> this country are destined to become progressively
> more severe in the future.[44]

This tentative conclusion had interesting rami-
fications for the economic interpretation of the twenties.
Clark speculated that the mildness of short-cyclical
contractions in the twenties might be closely related to
the severity of the final downturn. It seemed to him
that the surge of accelerated stimulus issuing from the
consumer durables industries had succeeded in carrying
general activity into abnormally prolonged expansion.
He noted that residential construction in particular had
advanced quite without regard for the first two 40-month
cycles of the twenties, and then began a decline early

---

[44]Ibid., 120-121.

in the third. This industry appeared to tend of itself toward longer more intense cycles than general business, and perhaps had heavily influenced the entire course of boom and bust in the decade. Perhaps the various consumer durables, with the aid of installment credit, had gained the primacy to compel overall expansion to the point where the inevitable accelerator reversal was felt in the durables themselves; then their contraction would undermine the prosperity they had so largely sustained. And finally, in depression, the general state of high consumer possession of durables might act as a serious obstacle to recovery, just as Rorty averred.[45]

The tenacity with which Clark explored and reiterated these themes in a work commissioned as a general one, was somewhat surprising. Yet he did discuss other sorts of factors. In fact he allowed that "non-cyclical" factors might have influenced very largely the great cycle of 1920-33. The dangerous international imbalances of the postwar era, which had come to seem basic to the most prestigious economists, also impressed Clark. At one point he stated that the Depression seemed "a phase of post-War dislocation even more than a cyclical

---

[45]Ibid., 27-33, 121.

decline."[46] He also stressed the role of the great
stock market speculation, and its inevitable crash, as
a major complicating factor. In addition Clark mentioned
that the rate of investment in fixed capital seemed
abnormally high in the 1920's, and might have contributed
to a new problem of technological unemployment. Several
other points were made in this portion of the book--a
chapter on "General Movements, 1922-29"--which left an
impression of broadly eclectic methodology.[47] Clark's
gravitation toward the financial and overinvestment-
oriented interpretation, which was central to the
eclectic interpretation of Wesley Mitchell, was clear in
this Chapter.

Yet although Clark had not resolved the question
of the relative weights of a variety of factors in the
severity of the Depression--the thrust of Strategic
Factors was unmistakable. Clark's concluding policy
recommendations centered on the need for stabilization of
expenditure on durable goods, of the producer and consumer types. For these durables, whatever the attendant
non-cyclical conditions, caused "intensified fluctuations"

---

[46]Ibid., 114. Clark had earlier suggested this,
though undogmatically, in his detailed and excellent
monograph, The Costs of the World War to the American
People (New Haven, 1931), 278-279.

[47]Ibid., 96-119.

through "mechanical relationships as inescapable as the laws of physics."[48] In such an economic system, Clark did not hesitate to assert, the goal of "balance" (as sought by experts under Hoover) seemed entirely chimerical--unless powerful new forms of intervention were instituted.[49]

With the publication of Strategic Factors, and the slightly earlier study by Mills, the Committee and the Bureau had sponsored a significant revision of New Era interpretation. And this was achieved without capitulation to the anti-business bias of institutionalism or the pro-business, investment-orientation of the economic orthodoxy. Mills had constructed a view hesitantly poised between the recent assumptions of the New Era and the neo-institutionalist critique of price rigidity. But Clark, developing the durable goods theme of Mills' work, presented a full and fresh formulation of the new strengths and weaknesses of the economy. Since

---

[48]Ibid., 191-192.

[49]Ibid., 127, 158, 226. Clark, now and later, felt that mere government spending, of the counter-cyclical sort he had advised in the twenties, would be useful but too superficial to control cycles. This was the conclusion of his full-scale study of The Economics of Planning Public Works (Washington, 1935); cf. p. 168. In this work, written for the Planning Board of F.E.R.A., Clark fully developed a concept of the "multiplier" effect of government spending, calling upon R. F. Kahn's essay of 1931, and other works, for help.

Clark's approach was designed precisely to explain protracted prosperity followed by abnormal depression, his
work culminated the tradition of intelligent New Era
optimism as well as providing an organically related
critical sequel. Clark's idea of the newly intense
expansion phase of the cycle was more dynamic, more convincing than the New Era ideas themselves had been.
These latter ideas had been largely attuned to slow-
moving, structural and institutional factors such as
rising wages and corporate mergers. Clark revealed more
volatile mechanisms of income-multiplication. In Clark's
hands the purely dynamic and cyclical approach to
economics achieved a higher synthesis, liberating it at
once from entanglements with traditional equilibrium
theory and with the almost traditional institutionalist
critique. If business cycle theory had provided a
fertile ground for mediation between these rival traditions, it now appeared to stake out a domain more
entirely its own.

It was a matter of handsome historical logic that
Clark at this juncture seemed to take intellectual, and
officially sanctioned, leadership. His work of the
twenties, more than Mitchell's, could be seen retro-
spectively to contain a veracious core of prediction.
His accelerator principle had perfectly embodied those
tendencies in New Era thought which had broached the

possibility of an economic dynamic elusive of institutional supervision. His emphasis on rising overhead costs had brought him to the verge of predicting larger business cycles, rather than the smaller ones that the neo-orthodoxy of managed "balance" was tempted to look for. The economic breakdown that occurred, of course, was not foreseen by Clark, and required that he develop his method still more powerfully. This he did by applying the accelerator method to consumer durables. In a sense Clark was applying the concept of overhead to the consumer laden with durable goods--investments similar to the capitalist's, often involving repayment of credit. But in making this readjustment of focus Clark further weakened the rooting of his work in institutionalist tradition. For now the selfish and short-sighted policies of the bosses of industry figured less largely in the origins of instability, the erratic behavior of the consumers more. If Clark were right, the superficial overlay of institutionalist notions in the New Era mind, such as the rough assumption that business had the power to control economic affairs--seemed overthrown. Clark's original formulation of the accelerator had partly worked against the prevalent assumptions that industrial wage and price policies were capable of regulating the relations of investment and consumption. His expanded application of the accelerator in 1934 left such possibilities utterly behind.

Hence, in Clark's formulation, the perspectives which were producing theoretical stalemate in the critique of the New Era were avoided. Clark was in accord with aspects of the work of Foster and Catchings and Stuart Chase, especially the orientation to the role of the auto and installment credit. But the notions of structural underconsumption due to low wages and high prices, or even simple market saturation, were not relied upon by Clark. On the other hand, Clark eschewed the orthodox idea of structural impediments to investment, especially as were supposed to inhere in high and rigid wage rates. Other non-cyclical factors, such as international financial derangement, Clark freely accepted as important in the Depression, as did the orthodox, the neo-orthodox, and to a lesser degree the underconsumptionist schools. Clark's approach had a special complementarity with the neo-orthodox writers such as Mitchell, Fisher and Keynes. As argued above, these men had emphasized financial crisis, and seemed to admit a new economic background of vulnerability to cumulative disruptions. But the origins of this new quality had been left obscure. The evident hankering of the neo-orthodoxy for a mediating and synthesizing approach to the basic problems of investment and consumption might have been largely satisfied by the work of Clark. Clark, partly in league with Mills, Rorty and the Bureau itself, had provided a full and feasible extension of neo-orthodox conception. It afforded great clarification of the astounding severity of the Depression in America; and it was conducive to the sort of extreme new remedial measures that were beginning to attract the major neo-orthodox figures. Though Clark's analysis dealt with great autonomous economic movements, it pointed, perhaps the more firmly, to institutional reformation.

CHAPTER IV

HANSEN, AND THE AMERICANIZATION OF KEYNES

As the 1930's wore on, the focus of economic interpretation inevitably moved away from the analysis of the boom and bust of 1921-1933 and toward the specific problems of the 1930's, viewed as a new age of depression. Interpretation of the prior cycle was coming to seem only part of the task of analysis, and often a part distinctly secondary to the question of what was wrong now. After the great recession of 1937-1938, the focus on the peculiar abnormalities of the thirties, of course, became still more engrossing. But The General Theory of Keynes, published in 1936, was already squarely oriented to the problems of prolonged depression and unemployment. As in the case of Keynes' Treatise of 1930, the background of English economic stagnation appears to have helped Keynes develop uncompromisingly critical perspectives. And in 1936, the sixth year of mass unemployment in America, conditions were prepared in many quarters for a quick acceptance of Keynesian premises. The most general innovative premise of Keynes' new work was that economic "equilibrium" might exist at low levels of activity. Keynes flatly opposed the classical assumption that economic activity tended toward a level of prosperous equilibrium.[1] However, Keynes wrote without fully clarifying his relation to the various schools of business cycle theory, which viewed economies as forever involved in cumulative movements and never quite attaining anything describable as equilibrium. Keynes' approach was somewhat static, and oriented to short-term analysis.[2] Yet it suggested critical possibilities even beyond most forms of dynamic cycle analysis; for with Keynes it simply was not assumed that depression tended to be followed by full revival and repetition of the cyclical process.

It has been mentioned that Rorty and Clark speculated that under their analysis contemporary depressions might involve a new ineptitude for revival, due to large stocks of durable consumers and producers goods. Keynes' approach, as we shall see, was compatible with this view, but was more excitingly oriented to the problem of chronic lack of investment per se. Traces of

[1]Cf. Lawrence Klein, The Keynesian Revolution (New York, 1949), 79-80.

[2]Cf. ibid., the later edition (New York, 1966), 195-196, 224.

such an approach--representing a sharp evolution of orthodox investment-centered attitudes--were increasingly appearing in the works of heterodox writers. The possibility of a radical exhaustion of investment outlets had been implied, as noted above, in Roosevelt's Commonwealth Club address. Stuart Chase had explicitly, if briefly, alluded to the matter in A New Deal. And the methodology of Clark seemed tacitly to assume that new outlets for investment would not appear in enough volume to offset the accelerator downswing which terminated one cycle, at least under modern conditions.

The ground, then, was being prepared in America so as easily to receive the Keynesian transplant. A good example of this preparation was provided by the progress of George Soule. In 1932 he held a structural underconsumptionist and rigid-price-oriented interpretation of the Depression. By 1934, in his far-ranging and provocative book The Coming American Revolution, Soule had importantly expanded his views. The typical heterodox blend of institutionalist and underconsumptionist criticism of business policies still dominated his outlook.[3] But now Soule gave a new emphasis to a temporary

---

[3]George Soule, The Coming American Revolution (New York, 1934), 146-149.

saturation of demand for housing and automobiles as leading the economy downward. Further, he added, perhaps
influenced by Mills' study, that reluctance of consumers
to replace durable and semi-durable goods had intensified
the Depression.[4] He went on to prognisticate powerfully.
Viewing NRA as the final business-sponsored eradication
of competition, he allowed that partial recovery of
profits and production might be expected. But full
revival he maintained was impossible. For prior overinvestment had been too great--and new forms of investment in consumers or producers durables had not material-
ized to replace the saturated outlets. Under these conditions a short boom in production of consumers goods
was under way, while heavy industry stagnated. Soule
added (showing knowledge of the accelerator principle)
that when consumption stopped rising investment would
actually decline, further depressing heavy industry.[5]
In a final fillip he speculated that should government
spending be employed to generate a more pronounced boom,
eventually this spending would be cut back. For
capitalism would be wary of levying sufficient taxes to
finance such spending. Then depression would reassert
itself.[6]

---

[4]Ibid., 154-155, 167.

[5]Ibid., 268-272.

[6]Ibid., 275-276.

Soule made these rather accurate predictions in the context of a heavily anti-capitalist and underconsumptionist vision. But like Chase, he had come to see that an appeal to technical, cyclical factors might enhance the underconsumptionist method. By 1934, thus, the logic of Clark's approach was exercising influence, even before Strategic Factors had made its mark. Further evidence of the advance of synthetic modes of thought was given by Soule's mention of the specific problems of investment. The assertion that great new products were not arising to provide channels for investment rounded out Soule's argument in an important way. It was a mere mention, of course, of what would become the basis of an entire school of Keynesian thought. In this sense, Soule's synthesis, like Chase's, was broad enough that it might be considered redundant. Into a bold framework of overinvestment-underconsumption, Soule introduced the subtler accelerator-based approach, and the whole question of lack of new outlets for investment. Perhaps Soule was guilty of over-explaining matters. In any case, radical interpretation was growing rounder and more pregnant with suggestion.

Then too, from the orthodox side, increasing preparations for the reception of Keynesian ideas were being made. Schumpeter in particular was to make a

fascinating contribution to American Keynesianism, even
in the course of his redoubtable resistance to it.
Schumpeter's first important expansion of his earlier
work on business cycles came in an article of 1935.[7]
There he restated his original claim that cycles were
based on the implementation of swarms of technological
innovation. Then he launched further propositions on
the history of business cycles, which would guide his
work till the completion of his two-volume study in 1939.
First he maintained that the historical pattern of business cycles consisted in the motions of three distinct
sorts of cycles simultaneously functioning. These
included not only the widely accepted 9 or 10 year
"Juglar" cycle and the roughly 3 year "Kitchin" cycle,
but also the controversial long cycle or "Kondratieff."
The existence of this latter cycle had been argued from
statistical evidence by the Russian economist
Kondratieff in the 1920's. Kondratieff saw the long
cycles, in both Europe and America, as eras of over 50
years divided into a period of buoyant prices and production and an ensuing period of relatively depressed

---

[7]Joseph Schumpeter, "The Analysis of Economic
Change," in Readings in Business Cycle Theory,
American Economic Association (Philadelphia, 1944), 1-19.
(Originally in Review of Economic Statistics, v. 17
May 1935, 2-10.)

activity.[8] Schumpeter now definitively accepted the Kondratieff cycles and correlated them with great episodes in technological history. The first long cycle had embraced the "Industrial Revolution" of 1783-1842; the second had its basis in the construction of railroads (and supporting industries such as steel) from 1842-1897; the third centered in the electrical, automotive, and chemical industries, and had accomplished its most expansive work from 1897-1929.[9]

Schumpeter, in fact, was not making really new claims. He drew on the work of Kondratieff, and even earlier ideas of the German Spiethoff and the Englishman D. H. Robertson. Alvin Hansen, in his 1932 book, had written a short but rich passage speculating that part of the severity of the Depression might be due to the convergence of downward phases of the three sorts of cycles. And Hansen considered Schumpeter already to have formed this opinion.[10] But as we have seen,

---

[8]Nikolai D. Kondratieff, "The Long Waves in Economic Life," in Business Cycle Theory, American Economic Association, 1944, 20-42. (Originally in German, 1926.)

[9]Schumpeter, "Analysis of Economic Change," 12-15.

[10]Hansen, Economic Stabilization in an Unbalanced World (New York, 1932), 93-100; on Schumpeter, 95. Schumpeter had, in fact, mentioned the convergence of the three cycles, as early as 1931, in an article on the Depression. But this was a minor theme with him till 1935. Cf. Joseph Schumpeter, "The Present World Depression: A Tentative Diagnosis," American Economic Review, v. 21, supp., March 1931, 197.

neither Schumpeter or Hansen had given much weight to
this possibility; both had dwelt on the non-cyclical
("non-economic" in Schumpeter's phrase) causes of the
Depression. Nor, finally, was Schumpeter outspoken on
the origins of the Depression in the article of 1935.
But here he formally inaugurated the central phase of
his career. This would entail an ultimately fairly
deterministic study of business cycle history, as based
on the movements of capital investment into technologic-
ally given outlets. And the more firmly Schumpeter
bound his conception of cycles (both the Juglar and the
Kondratieff) to the rise of great new industries, the
more he contributed to the idea that the Depression
grew from precisely a dearth of great new industries.
This latter concept was to form the heart of the interpretative application in America of the Keynesian theory
of the low-employment equilibrium.

How Schumpeter held the precarious balance
between his technological interpretation of economic
history and his "non-economic" interpretation of the
Depression--shall be described later, in connection with
his tomes of 1939. It was Hansen who came to lead in
the American reception of Keynes after 1936, and the
revision of orthodox attitudes toward the Depression.
The reason why Hansen did, and Schumpeter did not, make
this transition, appears to reside in a basic (though

after all, subtle) difference in their intellectual
constitutions. The two had in the early thirties been
in closest accord on the origins of the economic crisis.
Both had decried external impediments (especially in
international financial imbalance, and high wage rates)
to continuance of investment. But Hansen, while he
might have been fairly considered a member of the
Schumpeterian school of cycle analysis, was already in
1932 casting back for slightly more dynamic versions of
the investment-based theory of cycles. Thus he had
been attracted to aspects of the work of Spiethoff,
Robertson, Aftalion and others, which pictured the business cycle as a more fitful and erratic entity than had
Schumpeter.[11] Those earlier writers, seemingly daunted
by the deep economic depression of the 1890's, had
shown but wavering respect for classical notions of the
tendency to prosperous equilibrium. Their work had contained fragmentary, but clear, prefigurements of the
Keynesian reconstruction; and Hansen, in his Keynesian
phase, would make increasing reference to them. While

----

[11]Cf. above, on Hansen's book of 1932, p. 46.
On Spiethoff, and other early approaches to investment instability and stagnation, see Alvin Hansen,
Business Cycles and National Income (New York,
1964), Part III.

Schumpeter's greatest effort would continue to consist
largely in a kind of reining-in and regularization of
their ideas of the technology-investment cycle, Hansen's
would be to further loosen their conceptions, making room
for entire epochs of diminished investment. Hansen's
ruminations of 1932 in this vein had represented a line
of thought potentially quite different from the bulk of
his work of that year. Moreover, in that work he had
made mention of various other sorts of problems, such as
the role of luxury and durable goods. There was in
Hansen a kind of flexibility--even theoretical looseness--
which always held the promise of unorthodox departures.

In Hansen's original reaction to Keynes' General
Theory, an article of 1936, there may be found a kind of
crystallization of the preoccupations, both orthodox
and innovative, which guided Hansen's responses.
Further, in the course of the review, Hansen succeeded
in largely setting forth the bases of his own version of
Keynesian "stagnationism," later to dominate interpretation of the thirties in America. Hansen readily
accepted Keynes' notion of an "underemployment
equilibrium," and concentrated his energies on exploring
its origins and possible cure. Nor did Hansen doubt
Keynes' argument that the central determinant of underemployment was a decline in the "marginal efficiency of

capital" (the expected rate of profit on investment) to levels so low that interest rates do not commensurately decline, and do not direct savings into investment. And Hansen admired Keynes' discussion of "liquidity prefer- ence" (propensity to hoard cash) and how this tended in any case to put a lower limit on the fall of interest rates. Nor, finally did Hansen seem to object to Keynes' idea of a relatively fixed "propensity to consume," which partly influenced the efficiency of capital by setting the limits to the current market for production.[12]

Hansen had more to say on the question of what caused the abnormal fall in the efficiency of capital and the impulse to invest. Here Hansen combined two very different approaches. First he invoked the view of "current orthodox theory" that "institutional rigidities," supporting high wages and other costs, yielded a continu- ing adverse effect on the efficiency of capital. He asserted that the orthodoxy had very fully elaborated a theory of underemployment equilibrium in terms of these cost-price rigidities. These things Keynes had largely ignored.[13] Next Hansen offered a further explanation for

---

[12]Alvin Hansen, "Mr. Keynes on Underemployment Equilibrium," in Full Recovery or Stagnation? (New York, 1938), 20, 23-24. (Originally in Journal of Political Economy, v. 44 October 1936.)

[13]Ibid., 27-28. Keynes had not only ignored but controverted the orthodox position on wage rigidity as a

the decline in investment. He argued that the marginal
efficiency of capital might have recently undergone a
revolutionary fall due to changed historical and technological conditions. These might include decreasing
population growth, decreasing rate of technological
innovation, and/or decreasing rate of innovations
requiring large amounts of capital (such as railroads
and roads had required in the past).[14]

Hansen's point was, in truth, to indicate that
Keynes might have underestimated the forces working
toward underemployment. This had led, in Hansen's view,
to glibness in Keynes' proposals for combating stagnation. For Keynes had urged, in essence, that remedies
might be found in 1) the imposition of a regime of very
low interest rates, 2) income redistribution to raise
the propensity to consume, 3) socially controlled
investment. These means Keynes considered to be workable
within the framework of private enterprise. Hansen
simply doubted that enough of the three remedial policies
could be effected to bring prosperity without destruction
of capitalism. Monetary policy seemed simply too weak;

------

basis of equilibrium-at-low-levels. This position was
most identified with the English economist A. C. Pigou.
We will be studying it as it makes its way into more
specifically interpretative works, such as Hansen's own,
from 1932 on.

[14]Ibid., 28-30.

and the other two policies might threaten what remained of the drive to invest.[15] In any case, Hansen concluded that these policies would probably be increasingly implemented, and he seemed to know of no alternative.[16]

Hansen's position, despite its large remnant of orthodox argument, seemed already further advanced toward "secular stagnationism" than Keynes'. In the next two years the orthodox, institutionally-oriented elements of Hansen's view of the Depression would more and more recede. The thesis that the economy faced a dearth of outlets for investment would advance, and precisely along the lines Hansen set out in the 1936 review. What had been a very minor theme in his 1932 work, became dominant. And Hansen credited Spiethoff, not Keynes, for the pioneering. In discussing the brief portion of General Theory which dealt specifically with the business cycle, Hansen made this clear. He held that Keynes was following Spiethoff in viewing the cycle as chiefly governed by changes in the marginal efficiency of capital, and in maintaining that the collapse of the latter in depression might be greater than any possible movement in interest rates could correct. But on the matter of subsequent

---

[15]Ibid., 29-31.

[16]Ibid., 31-32.

economic revival, Keynes had emphasized the problems of the consumption of inventories and depreciation of existing fixed capital: the speed with which those things could be done would mainly determine the speed of recovery. With Spiethoff, the recovery of investment was primarily dependent on the development of new industries, products, resources.[17] Hansen clearly preferred this construction, and importantly differed with Keynes. Spiethoff was, at this point in time, surely no name to conjure with; Hansen was announcing that he himself would seek to strengthen Keynes' analysis of the failure of investment, by a sweeping appeal to the history of technology and resources.

Keynes had, in fact, made mention in the General Theory of the matters which Hansen connected with Spiethoff's work. In one passage Keynes alluded to the generally high marginal efficiency of capital in the nineteenth century--due to "the growth of population and of invention, the opening up of new lands, the state of confidence and the frequency of war."[18] This set of factors had over the long run tended to keep employment

[17]Ibid., 32-33.

[18]Keynes, The General Theory of Employment, Interest, and Money (New York, 1936), 307.

at reasonably high levels. Keynes went on to say that the contemporary, and probably the future, efficiency of capital was "much lower" than that of the nineteenth century, and dangerously lower than traditional rates of interest.[19] While Keynes did not here explicitly describe the causes of the weakening in the drive to invest, his perspectives were roughly conducive to the interpretation Hansen took.

Elsewhere in the General Theory Keynes made brief comments on the origins of the Depression in America and the world. Here again, Keynes generalized sketchily. He spoke at once of British and American conditions in the postwar period as exemplifying "an accumulation of wealth, so large that its marginal efficiency has fallen more rapidly than the rate of interest can fall."[20] Similarly, Keynes pictured the situation in the United States in 1929: new investment in the preceding years had been on "so enormous a scale" that prospective yield on further investment must have been at an "unprecedently low figure."[21] He took pains to deny that it had been a matter of absolute "over-

---

[19]Ibid., 307-308.

[20]Ibid., 219.

[21]Ibid., 323.

investment." His pragmatic point was precisely that under the conditions of 1929, efforts should have been made to support continued investment, both through lowering interest rates and through measures to raise the propensity to consume (such as income redistribution). Efforts in the latter direction would have maintained employment despite a lower volume of investment; and at the same time they would have averted the coming catastrophic fall of investment.[22] While Keynes denied that a state of over-investment, or even "full investment" had been reached, he clearly felt that such a state had been approximated. For he estimated, with a flourish, that could countries "so wealthy" as the United States or Britain maintain boom conditions continually, "full investment" might be attained within 25 years or less. That situation he boldly defined as one in which no further profit could be expected from additions to the stock of durable goods of any kind.[23] Such was the central theme of Keynes' aspirations for modern society—the end of "the scarcity of capital," entailing indeed the "euthanasia of the rentier."[24] To Keynes these

---

[22]Ibid., 323-324.

[23]Ibid., 323-324.

[24]Ibid., 375-376.

goals seemed very much within our reach; the marginal efficiency of capital was in decline largely due to the success of past investment. The problem now was to insure that investment might continue with enough strength to complete its work.

Keynes had, then, surely launched a thesis arguing the "secular stagnation" of investment as the economic challenge to this century. Yet in Hansen's hands, from the outset, the thesis was to be argued with a more concretely historical discipline, and with a difference. Hansen emphasized what Keynes seemed to take for granted: the absence of wholly new sorts of opportunities for investment. With Keynes, that aspect of the economic situation was subsumed under the fact of existing vast accumulations of fixed capital. Keynes and Hansen seemed in accord that in the nineteenth century new opportunities had been the keynote of economic activity. Hansen carried this analysis rigorously forward to the study of contemporary business cycles: if recovery was weak, new outlets must be inadequate. Keynes verged upon a view of the recent crisis as one brought on, and prolonged, by the great volume of prior investment itself. Thus, as noted above, Hansen had taken issue with Keynes' entire notion of business cycles.

Keynes was not highly concerned with specific historical or cyclical conundra. His labor had been to construct a model of the determinants of income and employment, which might, even under conditions of perfect competition, yield an underemployment equilibrium. As Lawrence Klein has said, elements of the Keynesian system abounded in the earlier thirties and even before then. Keynes was the first to put them together with elaboration and consistency.[25] Klein goes on to say that until Keynes had made his system, in traditional short-term equilibrium form, economists (he mentions Hansen) could not pursue any of the key possibilities it synthesized.[26] Yet Hansen had maintained a lively interest in past writings on the potential collapse of investment: and at the moment of his conversion to Keynes, Hansen, in fact, chose Spiethoff! From that time on, Hansen did, to be sure, go forth increasingly as an expounder of Keynesian theory and practice. But for the sheerly interpretative aspects of his work, Hansen was elaborating conceptions which were importantly at odds with Keynes'.

Still it is correct to speak of the Keynes-Hansen interpretation of the Depression. For Keynes and Hansen

---

[25]Klein, The Keynesian Revolution (New York, 1949), 42 ff.

[26]Ibid., 47-49.

were to lead the neo-orthodoxy to increasing acceptance
of the idea that investment was insufficient under current
conditions. And not by reason of institutionally imposed
distortions of the classical system of price-wage adjustment, but due to deeper, more autonomous factors affecting the whole nature of investment. Keynes and then
Hansen had finally freed themselves of the orthodox, and
even neo-orthodox and cycle-oriented, doctrine that outlets for investment were assured. Yet they maintained
that investment was the most potent determinant of
economic activity. Hence they transformed from within
the orthodox, investment-centered approach. That this
occurred seems entirely inevitable. Already in the early
thirties skillful unorthodox popularizers, like Chase and
then Soule, who instinctively gravitated toward anti-
business and underconsumptionist views, had felt
compelled to admit a largely separate problem of investment outlets. More generally, the accumulated discipline
of business cycle theory had weakened the intellectual
structure of neo-classical enonomics for the entire
profession. It could not have been very much after 1933
that full and free imagination would be given to the
matter of a cyclical depression that did not correct
itself.

Of course, Clark's accelerator approach, enhanced

by the focus on consumer durables, had already made a
frontal assault on this problem. And his work had
involved exposing the frailty of investment, as it
developed the theory of its interaction with consumption. But now, with attention shifting to the autonomous
motions of investment itself, further acts of synthesis
would be required if Clark's ideas were to survive. For
Clark had conceived of investment as largely subservient
to movements in consumption. Keynesian theory was not
only generally oriented to investment, but contained a
fully articulated concept of the "investment-multiplier."
Under this construction, income multiplication functioned
through an initial outlay for investment. This outlay,
as it found its way into the hands of the consumer (via
wages, salaries, or dividends), was productive of addi-
tional spending. The degree to which the original outlay
was multiplied depended upon the "marginal propensity to
consume" (prosensity to consume an increment of income)
of the society. Keynes considered this propensity to be
fairly fixed by habit and custom in a given country.
Hence the amount of aggregate investment which entered
the multiplying process was the vital variable, the
propensity to consume a rather passive agent.[27]

Hansen, in his original review of the <u>General</u>

---

[27]On the multiplier, etc., see Keynes, <u>General
Theory</u>, 113-131.

Theory, did not explicitly discuss the "multiplier." It probably was known to him much earlier through its originator R. F. Kahn, who had characterized its uses fairly fully in 1931.[28] Further, something like the multiplier had always been assumed by any investment-oriented economist. What Hansen stopped to comment upon, and to doubt, was Keynes' practical deduction from his model of the multiplier. This was that income redistribution, by raising the average marginal propensity to consume, would increase the multiplier and raise general activity. It was here, in policy recommendation rather than interpretation, that Keynes had joined the underconsumptionists. While he did not consider that problems in the sphere of consumption had been major causes of the decline of the efficiency of capital, he did feel that raising consumption would be an extremely useful way of bolstering investment. For, very simply, consumption always comprised a much larger percentage of total spending than investment. Thus a slight percentage rise in consumption would provide an overall stimulus as great as would a much larger (and hence less likely) percentage rise in investment.[29]

---

[28]R. F. Kahn, "The Relation of Home Investment to Unemployment," Economic Journal, v. 41, June 1931, 173-198.

[29]Keynes, General Theory, 325-326.

The theoretical ease with which Keynes shuttled
between investment and consumption, treating them as two
sides of an equation, naturally at first rattled Hansen
and other theorists of the investment-based approach.
For here were the most ambitious synthesizing elements of
the General Theory. And here the potential affinity for
the work of Clark was at its strongest. Still and all,
Clark's approach had already yielded a more dynamic and
balanced view of the interrelations of consumption and
investment. Clark had pictured the terrific cyclical
forces that had combined to produce the unique experience
of 1921-1933 in America. Clark had given consumption,
especially of consumers durables, a theoretical role to
match the historical development of the vast American
consumers' market. Keynes still wrote from a primarily
English point of view, holding that the role of consumption was only potentially dynamic.

By the same token, Hansen, while cleaving to the
Keynesian stress on investment, would render the concept
more dynamic, and more pertinent to American experience.
The fantastic development of new industries in America
from 1900 into the 1920's colored his views. It was in
this sense that the absence of commensurate new opportunities would be thematic to Hansen. Working with these
perspectives, Hansen (and in fact his major antagonist
in America, Schumpeter) would be drawn into the study of

concrete historical and technical factors, just as Clark had been. Although we do not think of Americans as peculiarly conscious of history, in this case they were forced to be. For economic experience had been recently so filled with appalling extremes, that the work of theory was rendered more exacting. An approach such as Keynes' which argued fairly glibly from capital wealth to stagnation of investment, seemed almost to leave out a stage of economic development: the stage which America, and not England, had just undergone in 1921-1933.

CHAPTER V

HANSEN, SCHUMPETER, AND THE DEBATE OVER
STAGNATION; CLARK BROUGHT FORWARD

With the appearance of Hansen's set of essays
entitled Full Recovery or Stagnation? in 1938, American
stagnationism achieved a quite full expression. Due to
the latest collapse of the economy in 1937-1938, Hansen
(Professor at Harvard after 1937) moved quickly to pre-
eminence as America's interpretor of Keynes and of the
Depression. So clear was the statistical failure of
investment throughout the thirties that Hansen was led
away from compromise with ideas less powerfully focused
on investment than his own. Price critique and wage
critique remained influential schools of thought, receiving further development and integration. But Hansen was
increasingly contributing to the decline of these
concerns, even though they continued to find a place in
his writings. On the other hand, he entered a more
direct dispute with Schumpeter, and others, whose view
of economic history was technology-and-investment based
like Hansen's own. Schumpeter saw no inherent technological obstacles to current investment, however, and

used a complex set of hypotheses to explain the severity
of the Depression. Then too, Hansen at the outset did
battle with a new viewpoint which integrated the
Keynesian multiplier and the accelerator principle. As
it turned out, resolution of this last controversy held
the likeliest key to compromise with Schumpeter's
compelling idea of modern technology. But, for the most
part, the urgency of Hansen's central argument repulsed
potential synthesis--even where it appeared tangibly to
develop in his own work.

It is peculiarly useful to study trends in
economic analysis through the work of Hansen. This is
due not only to Hansen's tenacious orientation to the
problems of concrete historical interpretation, rather
than to theory per se. He possessed related gifts,
which consistently led him to intelligent simplification
and generalization. Moreover, his avid reading in the
past and current writings in economics, and his confident commentary upon these readings, always gave his
work the quality of a fertile meeting-ground of ideas.
Many of the articles collected in Full Recovery or
Stagnation?, such as the abovementioned one on Keynes,
were in the form of reviews. Again and again Hansen
would discuss recent writings, and then relate them to
earlier ideas; here he would reassert his bias, calling

upon aspects of the work of Spiethoff, Aftalion, Robertson, Cassel, Wicksell, and Schumpeter.[1]

Hansen, for a short time, reserved his most critical tone for the business cycle theory of Oxford's R. F. Harrod, published in 1936.[2] This theory combined the accelerator and multiplier concepts, along with others. Hansen protested Harrod's stylistic arrogance; but he took pains to oppose the accelerator idea in particular. Hansen urged that, although the accelerator might play some role in business cycles, its importance was being overestimated in recent writings.[3] He went on to assert roundly that capital investment was capable of moving in irregular "spurts" quite irrespective of trends in consumption. Spurts of investment were ordinarily generated by "inventions, discovery of new resources,

---

[1]Cf. Hansen, Full Recovery or Stagnation? (New York, 1938), 51, 126, 320, etc. For even finer and more detailed reviews of cycle theory up to 1936, see Gottfried Haberler, Prosperity and Depression (rev. ed., Cambridge, Mass., 1958). We have not time to go into such detail, but must work with the authors who made the most forceful interpretative advances.

[2]Roy F. Harrod, The Trade Cycle (Oxford, 1936).

[3]Hansen, Full Recovery, 35-37, 49-51. (Originally an article of May 1937).
An example of early incorporation of the emphases of Clark's Strategic Factors, is Paul H. Douglas, Controlling Depressions (New York, 1935). Douglas' discussion gave about equal weight to underconsumption (via price and wage imbalances), accelerator effects, and the problem of consumer durables.

changes in the efficiency of factors of production, the 'swarming' of innovations."[4] As for a subsequent slow-down in investment, perhaps to the level required by mere replacement needs, Hansen denied that changes in consumption need be involved here either. He invoked the related approaches of Spiethoff and Keynes: with the most promising outlets exhausted for the time being, through recent expansion of the stock of capital goods, new investment falls off.[5] The difference in emphasis between Spiethoff and Keynes came in on the matter of depression and revival, as described above (was depression prolonged by the bulk of prior investment or by dearth of new outlets?). But for the turning point into depression, the two approaches combined powerfully, and in Hansen's view obviated resort to the accelerator formulation.

Harrod had rounded out his cycle theory with an explicit underconsumptionist element. He pictured the slowdown in the growth of consumption (required to bring on the accelerator decline in investment) as due to the following: during a boom prices and profits tended to rise abnormally, as competition grew more imperfect.

---

[4]Ibid., 51.

[5]Ibid., 50-52.

Hence the proportion of income entering saving rather than consumption rose. This was a traditional under-consumptionist construction; but with Harrod it needed only produce a diminution in the rate of increase of consumption. Then the accelerator slowed investment, and, in turn, the multiplier reduced income and consumption, launching the vicious spiral downward.[6] Hansen's salient criticism of this theory focused on its use of the accelerator. He held that even if in a boom consumption did not rise proportionately to savings, the rate of increase of consumption might be maintained, in absolute terms. And Hansen urged that accelerator theory made real sense only if it worked through changes in the absolute rate of growth of consumption--not the percentage rate. He felt that Clark himself had accepted this definition after an exchange of articles with the Norwegian economist Ragnar Frisch in 1931-32. Hansen then referred to a statistical and theoretical study of 1935 by Simon Kuznets, who was already emerging as the heir to Mitchell in rigorous empirical detachment. Kuznets argued that in reality investment had not normally followed movements in consumption with the precision required by the accelerator

---

[6]*Ibid*., 46-49.

theory.[7] Then Hansen moved into the statement of what in fact did primarily determine investment, as discussed above.

Nonetheless, in the later articles contained in _Full Recovery_, Hansen made certain brief but telling concessions to the Clarkian approach. As to Clark's realignment of accelerator theory toward the role of consumer durables, Hansen showed occasional interest. In the course of one of his explanations of how investment normally led economic revival after depressions--he

---

[7]The small, but growing, literature on accelerator theory was already very thorny. Since attempts to nullify the approach in the thirties failed, we will not go into detail. In any case, the major critiques of the accelerator, by Frisch, Kuznets, and Tinbergen, were not designed to eliminate it from cycle theory but only to suggest various cautions and limitations in its use. Frisch had been most dubious, and claimed to have dissuaded Hansen personally from his limited interest in acceleration as of the 1920's. As we have seen, Hansen and Mitchell had stopped including it in their analyses by the early thirties. The trend after Clark's work of 1934, despite the qualifications of Kuznets and Tinbergen and the hostility of Hansen, was toward increasing interest in acceleration (as Hansen complained). The articles in question were as follows: The series of exchanges of 1931-32 between Frisch and Clark, most importantly-- Ragnar Frisch, "Capital Production and Consumer-Taking-- A Rejoinder," _Journal of Political Economics_, v. 40, April 1932, 253-255; Clark, "A Further World," _ibid._, v. 40, October 1932, 691-693; Frisch, "A Final Word," _ibid._, October 1932, 694.
    Simon Kuznets, "The Relation Between Capital Goods and Finished Products in the Business Cycle" (1935), reprinted in Kuznets, _Economic Change_ (New York, 1953), 47-103.
    J. Tinbergen, "Statistical Evidence on the Acceleration Principle," _Economica_, v. 5 May 1938, 164-176.
    For Hansen's discussion, cf. _Full Recovery_, 48-50.

granted that "expansion in the demand for consumer durables" might be important, "since it involves a kind of investment financed partly from idle funds and partly from consumer credit."[8] He treated this as an interesting variation on the theme of the primacy of investment in the cycle. But it had been precisely the conclusion of Rorty and Clark that the rise of consumer durables gave consumption the cyclical volatility of investment. If the definition of investment had in fact become so loose, the nature of economics might have importantly changed since the days of Hansen's Spiethoff.

In the portions of Hansen's book which were written in 1938 with the specific intent of developing the "secular stagnation" idea, the consumer durables theme had grown larger. There Hansen stated, as a major characteristic of the contemporary economy, that "new capital outlay . . . is going, more largely than formerly, into consumers' capital."[9] In this, Hansen drew on the results of Kuznets' recent exhaustive statistical study on capital formation in America.[10]

---

[8]Hansen, Full Recovery, 125-126 (article originally printed in May 1936).

[9]Ibid., 309.

[10]Simon Kuznets, National Income and Capital Formation, 1919-1935 (New York, 1937).

Even in England, studies showed the major capital outlays
going for houses, roads, electricity, and public works--
all of which might "broadly" be considered consumers'
capital.[11] Hansen referred to these matters largely in
the course of emphasizing the relative weakness of the
more conventional outlets for capital, such as factory
plant and equipment.[12] In fact he went so far as to
characterize the American 1920's as weak in business
capital investment.

He listed the factors which had chiefly stimulated
prosperity in the 1920's: 1) residential building;
2) public works, financed often by state and local
deficits; 3) the large export surplus, financed by
foreign loans; 4) the "rise to full maturity" of the auto
industry; and 5) the burgeoning of consumer durable goods,
financed in part by installment credit.[13] Residential
building had boomed partly because of a postwar housing
shortage, and partly because of simple population growth.
Had these external supports been absent--as well as the
clearly external factors 2) and 3)--Hansen doubted that

---

[11]Hansen, Full Recovery, 308 (article originally
printed in April 1938).

[12]Ibid., 296-298.

[13]Ibid., 298.

the decade would have been a prosperous one.[14] He evidently considered categories 4) and 5) to have provided outlets to business investment as well as consumer durables purchases: but not enough of either to guarantee boom conditions. While Hansen was emphasizing an overall lack of secure outlets for capital, he was enumerating the developing outlets for consumer capital. He might have included under this heading factor 1) in addition to factors 4) and 5). Even factor 2), public works, Hansen might have considered consumer capital, according to his prior definitions.

In any case, aside from the question of consumer durables, Hansen came to a partial rapprochement with the accelerator theory itself. It was in his interpretation of the collapse of 1937-38, that Hansen made a dexterous application of the accelerator. First he set forth the background—the incomplete revival of investment in the recovery of 1933-36. Precisely because this short recovery had been based on increases in consumption, rather than a more normal surge of business investment, the accelerator came into play. Hansen described the recovery, truly under way by the winter of 1933-34, as primarily set off by renewed demand for consumer

[14]Ibid., 298.

durables and by income-stimulating federal expenditures.
As consumption rose due to these influences, investment
partially revived, "narrowly geared" to the servicing of
current consumption.[15] In the past, Hansen generalized,
investment had not followed, but led in revival, making
"a great forward thrust into new frontiers of technical
equipment and productive power."[16] But now in the 1930's,
with investment following consumption "like a dutiful
handmaiden," as soon as consumption ceased rising investment fell off to the level required by mere maintenance
of existing output. The "familiar principle of acceleration" came into operation "with full force":[17] but only
under the new conditions of secular weakness in investment.[18] The only hope for continuance of the recovery
was continued substantial government spending, to raise
consumption. However, the government had moved sharply
toward a balanced budget in 1937. At the same time the
boomlet in auto purchases was slowing, partly due to the
approach of "a saturation point in installment sales."[19]

---

[15]Ibid., 279 (article originally printed in
January 1938).

[16]Ibid., 279.

[17]Ibid., 281.

[18]Ibid., 281.

[19]Ibid., 282.

Hence the momentary stabilization in consumption, and accelerator collapse in investment.

Hansen, then, had clearly integrated the accelerator method into his characterization of secular stagnation of investment. But this latter concept remained the foundation of his analysis, the key to the difference between the 1930's and prior cyclical history. Earlier booms, had been led by investment which had "no relation to the then prevailing level of consumption":

> They were based instead on future expectations, on a dynamic conception of economic life. . . . The industrial revolution, the waves of railway construction, the booms based on electricity and automotive power had no relation whatever to the current volume of consumption.[20]

There had in fact occurred, in the 1890's after the railroad age, a "prolonged period of secular stagnation." Technology had brought on a remedy--the "electrical and automobile age" and attendant highway construction. This latter episode seemed clearly nearing completion by the 1930's, and, as Hansen put it, "nothing else of equal magnitude has so far appeared above the horizon."[21] Finally, in addition, the new fact of greatly diminished population growth appeared to further restrict the secular outlook for investment.[22]

---

[20]Ibid., 279-280.

[21]Ibid., 288-289.

[22]Ibid., 289.

Hansen's effort had been to place the Depression
of the 1930's in historical perspective. One result of
this effort was to leave his view of the great cycle of
1921-1933 in a state of fascinating indeterminacy. On
the one hand, he seemed to consider the boom of the
1920's as a great culminating wave of investment in autos,
roads and electrical-related products. On the other hand,
he explicitly imputed the prosperity of the 1920's to
"external stimulus" and non-business expenditure. The
two approaches were compatible, and in fact received
more balanced treatment in Hansen's (and others') work of
the 1950's.[23] The initial stages of the boom of the
twenties might be seen as based on a burst of investment--
ahead of consumer demand--especially in the auto and
electrical industries. The late stages of prosperity
might have been more largely stimulated by consumer purchases of durables, including cars and housing. But this
would imply that investment came to follow trends in con-
sumption--setting the stage for a vast accelerator contraction if consumption levelled off. Such a reversal
would of course involve the workings of Clark's original
accelerator concept, and his later idea of the accelerator pattern generated by purchases of consumer durables

---

[23]See below, pp. 211-219.

themselves. Hansen seemed extremely close to this sort
of formulation in 1938. He had applied the accelerator
broadly to the cycle of 1933-38; he had partly discussed
the 1920's as a boom in consumer durables. He only
omitted the final integrating step. This was because,
in describing the 1920's, he was attempting to discover
the origins of the dearth of outlets for business
investment, which was central to his view of the 1930's.
To explain, and remedy, the plight of the 1930's was
Hansen's goal. Hence he passed up opportunities for
refining his views on the era from 1920 to 1940 as a
whole.

In any event, Hansen had provided a close scrutiny
of historical conditions in the sphere of investment,
which Clark had rather ignored. While Clark had stressed
the highly cyclical pattern that could develop in an
economy centering upon consumer durables, Hansen emphasized the concommitant possibility of scarce outlets for
traditional producers durables. Hansen might have elaborated the implied relationships more. But he did supply
a plausible conceptual connection between the celebrated
energies of the economy of the 1920's and later stagnation. He held that the "great advance" in the productivity of manufacturing made during the twenties had been
accomplished without highly capital-intensive investments.

There was nothing wrong with technology: indeed its
sophistication made for innovations which were both labor-
and capital-saving.[24] This development Hansen evidently
considered to dovetail with the increase of purely consumer capital: but consumer capital could never adequately replace the expansive flow of (intensive) investors' capital, as it had functioned in past prosperities.
Hence in discussing the 1920's, as noted above, Hansen
had gone so far as to stress the temporary and unsound
nature of the boom. Now, in the aftermath of the
thirties, he considered that the outlets for both
producers' and consumers' capital were highly saturated
and unencouraging.[25] All this he maintained without
denying the vitality of the technology which had produced
the exciting new consumer durables and was improving
efficiency in an almost perpetual revolution.

There was a certain aura of paradox in these
claims--dynamic technology, stagnant investment--which
would bring Schumpeter, and others, into a corruscating
debate with Hansen over several years. This debate would
be so exacting in terms of the limited but difficult
problem of conventional investment outlets, that the

---

[24]Hansen, Full Recovery, 314-316.

[25]Ibid., 316.

perspectives of Clark would be partially eclipsed. The
fundamental lines of his argument--that the economy was
newly dynamic and cyclical due to voracious consumer
demand for durables, on top of perfectly lusty investment
in producers' goods--seemed largely inconsonant with the
preoccupations of the 1930's. Even the sequel to this
argument, the Rorty-Clark idea that depression under the
new conditions would prove unyielding to revival, seemed
a notion fit for 1932 or 1934. For the late 1930's
investigation was irrepressibly cast in terms of more
sweeping, epochal ideas. As Hansen put it in 1938, the
magnitude of the "problem of secular stagnation" might
well in the future "quite overshadow that of the business cycle."[26] Not the aftermath of the last cycle, but
the entire future of capitalistic investment was at
issue. That there was a parochial, or limiting, quality
to the focus on the outlook for investment was not readily
apparent to Keynes, Hansen, Schumpeter, and other economists. They had been sufficiently inculcated with the
investment-orientation of orthodox theory and early business cycle theory so that they considered a debate on the
fate of business investment tantamount to a debate on
capitalism. Furthermore, it was investment that was

[26]Ibid., 289.

showing the most alarming statistical failure in the
1930's. And so, after his close approximation to wider
synthesis with the accelerator approach of Clark,
Hansen's interpretative writings turned, for some time,
more flatly to the controversy over investment stagnation
per se.

Lending greater intensity to this controversy, of
course, were the questions of policy it entailed. Just
as Hansen had moved increasingly, from 1936 to 1938, to
concern with stagnation of investment outlets, he had
come to embrace wholeheartedly the need for government
action. His doubts as of 1936 that Keynesian policies
could revitalize capitalism were replaced by the conviction that they must be tried. This emerged clearly in
Hansen's discussion of the new collapse of 1937-38.
Investment had been timidly following consumption: continued recovery absolutely required that the government
go on spending. By 1938 conventional outlets for investment appeared so atrophied to Hansen that he roundly
recommended long-range government spending programs to
supplement it.[27] Hansen did not employ the laconic
Keynesian phrase "socially controlled rate of investment."[28] He simply propounded increased "public

---

[27]Ibid., 326-329.

[28]Keynes, General Theory, 325.

investment"; and, concluding Full Recovery, urged that
"We may thus learn that there is nothing incompatible
between the survival of private capitalism and a generous
admixture of public investment."[29]

While Keynes-Hansen arguments, on interpretation
and policy, appeared to take the initiative after 1936
and more so after 1938, other attitudes remained strong
and received new expression all along.[30] Both liberal
and orthodox criticism of institutionally imparted rigidities continued at a fairly high pitch. Nor did the
latter sort of critique ever wholly disappear from
Hansen's writings. It had been a dominant motif in his
work of 1932, overshadowing his concern with the autonomous fluctuation of investment. In the 1936 review of
Keynes the two themes were in equipoise, though
Hansen's interest was clearly gravitating toward the
latter. By 1938, and afterwards, the critique of

---

[29]Hansen, Full Recovery, 329.

[30]Hansen's influence may be readily seen in
Chapter 12 (on "Stimulating Investment"), in the
final Report of the Temporary National Economic
Committee. This committee had held broad Hearings on
the Concentration of Economic Power in America, from
1938 to 1941. The framework of the Hearings was
provided by the issue of monopoly, but Hansen's
stagnationism was already eroding that framework. Cf.
U. S. Temporary National Economic Committee, "Final
Report of the Executive Secretary," (Senate doc., 77th
Cong., 1st Sess.), (Washington, D. C., 1941).

rigidities occupied a minor but assured place in his
thought. He stated it strongly enough in 1938, pointing
to an economy "frozen with monopolistic practices all
around," in which our "productive resources, caught in
the straight-jacket of an inflexible price structure,
are unable to find full employment."[31] He went on,
interestingly, to speculate that this situation might be
the result of the new restriction of investment outlets.
Industries which had lost their expansive drive might
naturally begin to conspire against the forces of competition.[32] Aside from these considerations, Hansen still
held an uncompromising position against high and rigid
wage rates. The orthodox maxim that raising wage rates
raises costs and thus deters investment, Hansen still
considered a prime lesson of the Depression experience.[33]
Summarizing on the problem of high costs, he found the
latter responsible "in large part" for the failure of
investment in the 1930's. The blame he placed upon corporate price policies, labor policies, and government
policies such as N.R.A.[34] Thus, concentrating upon the
effects of price and wage rigidity on investment, Hansen

---

[31]Ibid., 299 (article of April 1938).

[32]Ibid., 299.

[33]Ibid., 287 (article of January 1938).

[34]Ibid., 286.

easily incorporated the institutionalist perspective into
his view of overall investment stagnation. Steering
strictly away from any notion of underconsumptionist
effects due to price rigidity, he made this part of his
analysis consonant with orthodox economics.

This sort of construction occupied a more central
place in the works of economists who denied that any
inherent lack of investment outlets existed. An important example of this line of interpretation in post-
Keynesian America was provided in 1937 by Sumner Slichter.
Slichter was a professor of "business economics" at
Harvard after 1930, and one of the most influential
academic economists of the period from the twenties to
the present. Slichter's article of 1937 had been prepared
at the request of the editors of the Review of Economic
Statistics, including Schumpeter, Gottfried Haberler, and
Seymour Harris--all spokesmen for the essentially orthodox
outlook. Slichter at first urged that business cycle
theory must cultivate flexibility in its approach to
historical interpretation. In discussing the turning
point of 1929, Slichter was receptive to the accelerator
construction, and even to broader ideas of overproduction
and underconsumption.[35] But when it came to the unique

---

[35]Sumner Slichter, "The Period 1919-1936 in the
United States: Its Significance for Business-Cycle
Theory," Review of Economic Statistics, v. 19, February
1937, 13.

severity of the ensuing Depression, Slichter warned that
one's notion of the prior turning point was of little
weight. Not concepts of the business cycle, but broader
historical conditions must be consulted. These he found,
just as had orthodox economists in the early thirties, in
international financial imbalance and crisis, and the
strange new rigidity of wage rates. The resistance of
industrial prices to decline, relative to raw material
prices, had been a complicating factor. But Slichter did
not consider this a result of monopolistic tendencies,
but rather a result of the efforts of Hoover and of business itself to maintain high wages. Financial turmoil
and high wages conspired to destroy the incentive to
invest. True lack of outlets seemed not to embody even
a plausible basis for such a collapse in investment. New
Deal policies, including efforts to raise consumption and
prices, and budget deficits, were simply wrong. They
were not directly supportive enough to investment: hence,
even with profits rising after 1933, investment failed
adequately to recover.[36]

Such was the adamancy of orthodox investment-
based analysis, carrying forward the critique of external,
institutional conditions from the New Era to the period

[36]Ibid., 14-16.

of the middle New Deal. Nor was liberal institutionalism
relinquishing its original formulation. One of the more
ambitious reinforcements of the perspectives of Berle and
Means was supplied by Arthur R. Burns in his Decline of
Competition of 1936. Burns was a professor of economics
at Columbia after 1928, and worked in various other
research and advisory capacities. In Decline of Competition, Burns dwelt more on the market practices of big
business than on its organizational structure, as treated
in the 1933 work of Berle and Means. Burns held that the
dominant corporations had the power to resist price cuts,
and the incentive to do so, since their investments had
been "excessive in relation to output."[37] The new
industrial regime of the 1920's had seen to it that
prices had stayed high enough to divert the gains of productivity to profits, more than to rising wages. Hence,
over-saving, over-investment, and underconsumption.[38]
This was the same amalgam of institutionalist price
critique and underconsumptionist deductions employed
earlier by Tugwell, Foster and Catchings, and others.

---

[37]Arthur R. Burns, The Decline of Competition
(New York, 1936), 142.

[38]Ibid., 264-266.

To support this view of the origins of the crisis,
Burns had to deal with a study of industrial capacity put
out by the Brookings Institute in 1934. This study had
concluded fairly authoritatively that there was "no
evidence of any real trend" toward overcapacity of
industrial plant in the 1920's. Rather, it was estimated
that industry had run at a fairly even average utilization
of capacity of 80%, from 1925 to 1929: nor did this
appear to differ with conditions in the prewar economy.[39]
Burns, as did some others, doubted that statistics could
entirely establish these matters. But, even granting the
truth of the study's conclusions, Burns urged that fundamental excess of capacity might have developed. He argued
that the trend to overcapacity need not be revealed during prosperity, since consumer demand might expand enough
to veil it. The revelation of prior overinvestment and
underconsumption would occur in the intensity of the
Depression that followed.[40]

In this, Burns verged upon saying merely that _if_
consumption had been higher and investment lower, _then_

_____

[39]Edwin G. Nourse et al., America's Capacity to
Produce (Washington, 1934), 416-425, 297.

[40]Burns, Decline, 267.

the Depression would have been less severe. He might,
for example, have appealed to Keynes here: but not to
argue that a state of absolute overinvestment relative to
consumption had obtained. If in fact production at 80%
of capacity was normal for modern capitalism, Burns
ought to have brought other factors to his explanation of
the actual severity of the Depression of 1929 to 1933.
Interestingly, although Burns clung to the simple overinvestment interpretation, he did in one place elaborate
another approach. He showed the influence of the
National Bureau and the Mills-Rorty-Clark idea of consumer durables in the Depression. He described how
products whose replacement may be postponed, such as
cars, had suffered production declines in the Depression
far greater than other consumer goods. He went on to
urge that had the prices of these goods been cut more,
their production might better have been maintained.[41]
(He pointed out that auto prices had fallen far less
than those of textile products, auto production far
more.) In this fashion he attempted to absorb the new
consumer durables problem into the price-oriented method
of analysis. The suggestion of a problem independent of
his frame of reference remained for the reader to ponder.
Still and all, Burns had demonstrated the continued

[41]Ibid., 252, 262.

viability of the anti-business, price-based interpretation. Partly because it still relied on "if's," new
statistics and new ideas had failed to overthrow its
premises. And though Burns' work may have shown
resistance to fruitful newer lines of approach, he certainly made his interpretative case in more relevant,
developed ways than had Berle, Means, and Tugwell in
1933.[42]

A still weightier addition to the price (and wage)
critique was made in 1936 by Frederick Mills' Prices in
Recession and Recovery, sponsored by the National Bureau
and the Committee on Recent Economic Changes. Mills'
work, primarily a detailed statistical study of prices,
carried forward his earlier theoretical contribution to
price critique and to other orientations. Just as he had
earlier, Mills set forth the view of prices as newly
inflexible, due to rising overhead costs, trade agree-
ments and other factors.[43] But now Mills took time to

[42]Other contributions to liberal price critique
in the middle thirties were Gardiner Means, "Notes on
Inflexible Prices," American Economic Review, v. 26,
March 1936; and Arthur Adams, Analyses of Business Cycles
(New York, 1936). An interpretation fully uniting
liberal price critique with analysis of financial
imbalance, was Arthur D. Gayer, Monetary Policy and
Economic Stabilization (London, 1935).

[43]Frederick C. Mills, Prices in Recession and
Recovery (New York, 1936), 42.

elaborate the inner workings of these tendencies. He
saw, for the most part, the very trend toward high
industrial prices to accentuate the inflation of overhead costs. It was a self-reinforcing process: high
prices of producers' goods raised overhead costs in
industries using them--and so on in an inter-industry
chain of effects which left all fabricated producers'
and consumers' goods inflated in price.[44]

Mills' interpretative conclusions included various extensions of this approach. From the investment
side, after 1929 the high volume of new capital equipment, much of it "constructed under conditions of
exceptionally high cost," became "a major factor in the
problem of readjustment."[45] As to consumption, the relative rise of fabricational prices left the producers of
raw materials and the consumer in general increasingly
at a disadvantage. Interestingly, Mills excepted factory
labor from this spreading plight. Rather, factory labor
had made, along with business, disproportionate gains in
the prosperity of the twenties. High wages had in their
turn contributed to rising costs of production, and hence
eventually come to deter investment.[46] Labor had been in

---

[44]Ibid., 42, 59, 351-352.

[45]Ibid., 59.

[46]Ibid., 351, 462.

an unusually strong position due to wartime gains and the
subsequent restriction of immigration.[47] But Mills meted
out blame for both mistaken wage and price policies to
business, government and labor.[48] In any case, Mills'
idea of the genesis of the regime of high costs included
interacting stimuli from all industrial prices and
industrial wages as well. These high costs had worked to
choke off investment directly, and through prohibitive
prices of the consumers' goods offered to the broader
non-industrial community. Furthermore, much of Mills'
discussion went to show that these influences had continued to operate in preventing normal revival in 1933-
1936. High costs and prices, together with their tangible
legacy of accumulated, costly capital equipment--consti-
tuted formidable obstacles both to the continuance of
prosperity in the 1920's and to later recovery.[49]

Mills adverted briefly to the independently
depressing influences of national and international
financial crises.[50] He also treated, as he had in 1932,
the new problems of durable goods. Here Mills' interest

---

[47]Ibid., 65.

[48]Ibid., 464.

[49]Ibid., 387-391, 462-463, 465-466.

[50]Ibid., 42, 388.

seemed somewhat diminished; and he made an effort to draw
this problem into the context of price critique. Mills
stated the idea that demand for durables (consumers' and
producers') suffered peculiar attrition in hard times.
Then, just as Burns did, he moved to emphasize the relative price rigidity of durables and the role this might
have played in discouraging their purchase. Mills con-
jectured that relative rigidity might have developed in
durables prices due to strong monopolistic tendencies in
durables industries. In any case, he considered that
price flexibility would provide an important corrective
to troubles in these industries and others which produced
goods of elastic demand.[51]

It may be seen that Mills' study of 1936 had
combined with unusual depth the orthodox critique of high
wage costs, and the underconsumptionist critique of high
prices. The detail of the argument, and the wealth of its
statistical demonstration, made the work a redolent
synthesis in the methods of institutionalism. Industrial
prices and wages were yoked in Mills' view, and the
matters of overhead and durables at least largely contained in the critique of institutional forces and
policies. However, the underconsumptionist theme seemed

---

[51]Ibid., 381-383, 466.

partly compromised by the emphasis on high wages. After
all, the method of underconsumptionism had centered for
years upon the relative backwardness of wage rates. The
dangers of a transfer of purchasing power from farmers,
professionals, and others to labor and management, Mills
did not elaborate convincingly. Thus, the brunt of
Mills' work may have gone to strengthen the case of the
more orthodox or investment-oriented economists.
Certainly Hansen's use in 1938 of the price/wage-rigidity
motif, was entirely to the end of proving impediments to
investment. Of course, the more pro-business economists,
such as Slichter, still hewed mainly to the wage critique--
the more liberal, such as Burns, to the price critique.
But Mills had made a signal contribution to the evolving
centrist tradition of orthodox analysis. This was the
school to which Hansen had referred in 1936 as offering
a fully formulated alternative to Keynes, an approach to
underemployment equilibrium through institutional inflex-
ibilities. That Hansen came to incorporate this method
into, and subordinate it to, Keynesian stagnationism, was
proof of the synthesizing energy of Hansen. More orthodox economists would consider that the price/wage explanation of underinvestment could stand alone. Their debt
would be to Mills' statistics, and his construction of
them, more than to any other interpretative work. The

complete interpenetration of orthodox analysis and institutionalism was well under way.

In Mills, and in Hansen, the critique of high
costs bore most pointedly upon conditions in the construction industry. Mills' statistics indicated that basic
materials and labor costs in the construction industry
had moved in such a way as to leave them "prohibitively
high" at the beginning of recovery in 1933.[52] One of
Mills' charts showed that construction costs, very high
in 1929, were still higher (relatively to other prices)
in 1933.[53] Hansen in turn stressed these matters in his
discussion of the failure of residential housing
construction in the Depression. Hansen considered that
had a boom in housing occurred in the thirties, recovery
might have been much more normal. But the decline of
population growth, and high construction costs, had
combined to prevent such a boom.[54] Though even here
Hansen by no means held cost rigidity a sufficient
explanation of developments, he made his most specific
use of Mills' method.

In the controversy over Hansen's more fundamental

[52]Ibid., 365.

[53]Ibid., 368.

[54]Hansen, Full Recovery, 298-300.

theory of stagnation of investment outlets, variants of
the price/cost critique were surely not to play the only
opposition parts. In 1939 Schumpeter completed his vast
and complex contribution to interpretation. The two-
volume Business Cycles expounded the theory and history
of business cycles over the past century and a half, in
the United States, England, and Germany. Schumpeter
dwelt at length on the recent material, and developed
explicit arguments against Hansen's stagnationism as well
as other schools of thought. Opposition to Hansen
seemed perhaps most urgent to Schumpeter; at the same
time the area of methodological affinity between the two
men was great. For Schumpeter's work crowned the
technological interpretation of economic history--the
very tradition which Hansen had invoked.[55]

---

[55]On Schumpeter, see the fine set of essays by
leading economists, Seymour Harris, ed., Schumpeter--
Social Scientist (Cambridge, Mass., 1951). These
writers, with little exception, agreed that the breadth
and power of Schumpeter's economic history made comparison with Marx unavoidable. Schumpeter himself felt
deepest affinity with Marx, even though he felt no
revolutionary promptings. As to the Business Cycles, in
one of the abovementioned essays Arthur Smithies of
Harvard called it the greatest intellectual effort
ever made in the unification of history, theory, and
statistics. Cf. Schumpeter, 21. (This writer agrees:
we are dealing with the Capital of our century.)

Now Schumpeter made a sustained, and fantastically articulated, application of the three-cycle schema he had described in his article of 1935. One of the successes he claimed for this system was its exact prediction of a major depression in 1929 to 1933, due to the convergence of the contraction phases of all three cycles. Hansen had considered this important to Schumpeter's approach as early as 1931; but now Schumpeter gave his first interpretative elaboration of the idea. The first principle of the interpretation was that in the 1920's the economy had entered upon the "Kondratieff downgrade." This Schumpeter described as the phase of the technological long cycle connected with the "completion"--including quantitative and qualitative development--of the major innovations of that long cycle. The current long wave or Kondratieff, dating from the turn of the century, had its basis in electrical, automotive, and chemical innovations. Hence, the "downgrade" would be based on intense, completing developments in those fields. Schumpeter held that a number of circumstances ought to have--and had in fact-- accompanied this process by the 1920's. Competitive strain ought to have been great as the new industries came of age, exercising maximum displacing pressure on older industrial patterns. Such was the case, Schumpeter urged, pointing to the awkward position of

the old coal and railroad industries in the 1920's.[56]
Furthermore, these conditions were linked, through
relentless raising of productivity, to rising real wages
and a great general consumer prosperity.[57] Schumpeter
quoted Mills' study of 1932, which showed that both
absolute and _per capita_ output had increased at a
higher rate in the twenties than in the period from 1901-
1913.[58] All had been as theoretically expected in this
phase of the Kondratieff. And so, when the shorter
cyclical movements (the Juglar and the Kitchin) began
their contraction phases, was the subsequent Depression
particularly intense. For the prosperity had been of the
sort which released "an avalanche of goods smashing its
way through the resisting framework of the existing
industrial structure."[59]

Schumpeter, then, had employed the three-cycle
schema (particularly his characterization of the phases
of the long cycle) to heighten and to complement his
original dynamic conception of the business cycle, first
outlined in 1911.[60] By the same token, he had largely

---

[56]Joseph Schumpeter, _Business Cycles_, (New York,
1939), v. 2, 753-755.

[57]_Ibid._, 795, 824-837.

[58]_Ibid._, 795-796.

[59]_Ibid._, 792.

[60]See above, p. 32.

reversed himself on the origins of the severity of the
Depression, which he had at first connected with external
or "non-economic" factors. It should be apparent that
his new, more dynamic and cyclical approach provided a
powerful amplification of the views of the dominant
interpretors in the twenties, especially Mitchell.
Schumpeter wholly preserved the sense of awe felt by
Mitchell in 1929, in contemplating the pace of industrial
and technological competition, and expanding consumption,
during the twenties. Mitchell's minor doubts as to
whether the strains and disparities of such an intense
boom could be taken in stride--became, in Schumpeter's
reconstruction, a certainty that violent depression must
follow. Not just one exciting cycle, but the jarring
culmination of "the industrial revolution of the preceding thirty years," had been at issue in the 1920's.[61]

Schumpeter elaborated this conception, criticizing all schools and forms of objection, orthodox or
heterodox. All the qualities of the experience of the
twenties he explained as inevitable aspects of the
Kondratieff downgrade in a robustly functioning capitalism. The word "downgrade" derived most clearly from the
price level, slightly falling during the twenties. This,

---

[61]Schumpeter, _Cycles_, v. 2, 794.

of course, Schumpeter connected with inter- and intra-
industry competition, as new products and processes came
to maturity.[62] Evidences of business movement toward
monopolistic policies, Schumpeter, with typical transforming energy, viewed as a kind of proof of the harrowing competitive pressures of the period.[63] Discussing
the various statistics on profits, he maintained that
profits had been low in the twenties (particularly profits
in relation to total assets). Again he was in accord
with Mitchell's views as of 1929. Notions of "profit
inflation" he found absurd, as well as impossible under
the conditions of competitive Kondratieff downgrade.[64]
Wages he found to have been high in the postwar period,
and rising. But abandoning his earlier more orthodox
view, he saw no reason why this should have impeded business. High wages had merely encouraged labor-saving
innovation; a special result of this, to be sure, had
been fairly high technological unemployment. But again,
these things he maintained had always formed a part of
historical developments in the later, more competitive
stages of the long cycle.[65] Moreover, the depressed

---

[62]Ibid., 809-810.

[63]Ibid., 802.

[64]Ibid., 832.

[65]Ibid., 837-839.

state of agriculture, so commonly viewed as a dangerous postwar legacy, Schumpeter considered to have had deeper roots in the vital improvement of agricultural technology.[66]

Having recast the elements of the New Era approach into a fully cyclical vision, Schumpeter derived the severity of the Depression directly from the intensity of prior advance. But though this derivation was at the heart of his interpretative method, he stopped to consider subordinate questions. He unhesitatingly brought into his interpretation the early-Depression emphasis of the National Bureau, the Mills-Rorty-Clark view of consumer durables. Just as Hansen had, Schumpeter used Kuznets' statistics to demonstrate that business investment had been importantly supported in the 1920's by consumer investment in durables. He used this information to refute the schools of thought which had considered simple "overinvestment" a major cause of the crisis.[67] He was not, of course, tempted by Hansen's conclusion that business investment had actually been moribund in the twenties. Rather he took precisely the route Mills and Clark had laid out: he held that the increasing role of consumer durables imparted a heightened cyclicality to

---

[66]Ibid., 738-839.

[67]Ibid., 801.

the economy.[68] He went on to deride interpretations
which sought the origins of the Depression in over-
saving or underconsumption: instead the twenties had
seen an accentuated drive to consumption, and allied
phenomena such as installment debt.[69] But he granted
that consumer durables purchase might be expected to
rise in prosperity and fall sharply in depression.
This, and the related matter of consumer indebtedness,
he considered had introduced special destabilizing
influences into the otherwise normal American
Kondratieff.[70]

Schumpeter made these points clearly but briefly.
He used them to help explain why a necessarily vast
Depression had taken on still greater dimensions. He
could not, however, go so far as Clark had gone, in
seeing the severity of the Depression as a function of
the new problem of consumer durables. For Schumpeter's
aim was precisely to characterize the Depression as a
fundamentally normal and precedented reaction to far-
reaching capitalist innovation and progress. He stressed
that there was nothing historically novel in the advances

---

[68]Ibid., 801.

[69]Ibid., 824-825.

[70]Ibid., 824-825, 909.

of the twenties or the retreat of the thirties.[71] He
granted, as in the case of durables, that there had been
several aggravating influences in the Depression. The
other influences he discussed were the abnormal movement
of stock prices in 1928-29, and the peculiar weakness of
the American banking structure, based on small, fairly
independent units.[72] International imbalances he now
described as distinctly secondary aggravations, at least
in the American case.[73] Whether he described such compli-
cations with greater or lesser emphasis, he sought to
bring them into his broader historical perspectives.
Here was his point, described in his perfectly inimitable
way:

> Capitalism and its civilization may be decaying,
> shading off into something else, or tottering
> toward a violent death. The writer personally
> thinks they are. But the world crisis does not
> prove it and has, in fact, nothing to do with it.
> It was not a symptom of a weakening or a failure
> of the system. If anything, it was a proof of
> the vigor of capitalist evolution to which it
> was—substantially—the temporary reaction. And
> in any case it was—again substantially—no
> novel occurrence, no unprecedented catastrophe
> expressive of the emergence of new factors, but
> only a recurrence of what at similar junctures
> had occurred before.[74]

---

[71]Ibid., 797, 925-927.

[72]Ibid., 903, 909.

[73]Ibid., 937-938.

[74]Ibid., 908.

What was menacing capitalism Schumpeter located
in the 1930's, in the period of incomplete recovery
rather than in the initial contraction. Naturally, it
was here that Schumpeter turned most directly to the
repudiation of Hansen's stagnation thesis. At the outset,
Schumpeter conceded the plausibility of a trend toward
exhaustion of outlets for investment. He further noted
that the increase of capital-saving innovations, discussed
by Hansen, was in fact a potential cause for concern.[75]
But at this point Schumpeter brought to bear the full
weight of his historical judgement. He considered it
simply senseless to argue that a full crisis in outlets
for investment could have developed so quickly--and so
hard upon a prosperity as pronounced as ever had been
experienced.[76] Moreover, substantively speaking,
Schumpeter held that in truth plenty of investment opportunities remained in the electrical, automotive, chemical
and other industries. The great completing processes of
the current Kondratieff were not at an end; and they
underlay what there had been of a (Juglar) recovery in
the thirties.[77]

---

[75]Ibid., 1034.

[76]Ibid., 1036-1037.

[77]Ibid., 1021.

The "vogue" of the stagnation idea Schumpeter considered understandable in the wake of poor recovery and the collapse of 1937-38.[78] But Schumpeter's own explanation of the undisputable deficiency of investment was the tempestuous social and political climate of the American 1930's. Not so much what had been done-- Schumpeter considered that the New Deal may not have affected the general course of the economy terribly much either for good or ill--but what had continually been threatened.[79] Most vivid was the example of the electric utilities, where obvious opportunities for large investment seemed to have been passed over due to the possibility of government takeover.[80] More generally, Schumpeter pointed to the currency of angry talk against "monopoly," and the equation of the latter with "big business." In England an anti-business atmosphere had developed gradually over decades. Schumpeter contrasted the American experience: the suddenness of the change in public opinion might have warranted a stunned retreat of investment funds.[81]

---

[78]Ibid., 1033.

[79]Ibid., 1043.

[80]Ibid., 1043.

[81]Ibid., 1047.

In the early thirties Schumpeter had meant to embrace by the term "non-economic" all the influences of institutional and governmental policies. An interesting evolution of his attitude now brought him largely to exclude concrete acts of policy from the basic chain of economic causation. This seems to have left his interpretation of the 1930's somewhat weakened-- or perhaps open to the same charge of discontinuity, or overly sharp separation of eras, which he had levelled against Hansen. In any event, Schumpeter now provided some lively rebuttals of institutionally oriented interpretation, orthodox and unorthodox. First, while he viewed New Deal wage-raising policies as unwise, he concluded that high wages, in the 1930's as well as the 1920's, had not fundamentally impeded investment.[82] Technical advance had probably achieved sufficient offsets to higher wages all along.[83] In maintaining this, the most prestigious guide to orthodox opinion brusquely shunted aside the cornerstone of orthodox interpretation. Second, as to relative rigidity of industrial prices before and after the crash, Schumpeter shrugged. Liberal critics had failed to note that high and rigid wage rates had played an essential part here: farmers

---

[82] Ibid., 1011, 1042.

[83] Ibid., 1042.

could "take the cut" both as laborers and as operators, hence were simply freer to compete.[84] As to the capital goods industries, there was no point in their entering serious price competition, since demand for their products was feeble and unresponsive.[85]

This last argument represented a powerful antidote not only to Mills' position on producers' goods and construction prices, but also to Mills' and Burns' idea that price rigidity had restricted consumption of consumer durables. Neither their nor Schumpeter's viewpoint could be definitively verified. Perhaps the truth lay between the two positions; but once again liberal price critique was on the defensive. Of course, the construction so fortified by Mills' study was the combination of both price and wage rigidity as the basis of general industrial price rigidity. Schumpeter emphasized the wage factor in this, and to that extent cleaved to the orthodox intuition, as had Slichter. But he roundly denied that wage or price rigidity were ample grounds for an "interpretation" of the severity of the

[84]Ibid., 948-949.

[85]Ibid., 949.

Depression or the niggardliness of recovery.[86]

Schumpeter's work was probably the first so spiritedly to controvert all other going interpretation. It contributed, with the key emphases of Clark and Keynes-Hansen, to the overthrow of institution-centered approaches. This was true even though Schumpeter's ultimate explanation of the length of the Depression embodied a kind of hyper-sensitive rarification of earlier (orthodox) institutionally based interpretations. The mere political climate was to replace the somewhat more substantive issues of New Era and New Deal policies. Nonetheless, the initial, and epochal, onslaught of the Depression Schumpeter characterized as engendered by pervasive and irremediable forces. As much, or more, than Hansen, Schumpeter calibrated his view of 1929-33 to autonomous movements, particularly of investment.

Still and all, of course, Schumpeter's concept of the cycle, even the long wave, was founded on that irreducible combination of institutionalism and invest- ment theory which had originated in Schumpeter's early work, and had influenced Mitchell in the 1920's. In this

---

[86]Ibid., 954. Support for Schumpeter's conten- tion had recently been supplied by Edward Mason, who argued from statistics that price rigidity had not increased since the turn of the century. Cf. Edward S. Mason, "Price Inflexibility," Review of Economic Statis- tics, v. 20, May 1938, 53-64.

view technological history interacted with the competitive institutional structure of capitalism to bring on cycles. Earlier we called this view an adaptation of institutionalism and classical equilibrium analysis.[87] We also described another element which had entered this compound in the New Era, including Mitchell's writings: the offsetting function of high levels of consumption. Why should the competitive introduction of new products and processes lead to reversal if consumption continued rising buoyantly? Schumpeter, precisely as had Mitchell, considered the 1920's a time of vast labor and consumer prosperity. Mitchell had moved from this view of fundamentals-in-balance to an interpretation of the Depression based on relatively external financial factors. Now in 1939, after years of labor, Schumpeter saw fit to develop the possibility that massive maladjustment could evolve in industrial markets despite unimpeded consumption. Schumpeter's _tour de force_ contained a suggestion of paradox. Impressionistically speaking, of course, the very germ of his interpretative position--that the depth of the reaction grew from the intensity of prior advance-- was redolent of paradox.

One relatively detached element in Schumpeter's construction, however, may have boded resolution. This

---

[87]See above p. 33, note 33.

was his uncompromised allusion to the new problem of consumer durables. At one point, in the course of his
rebuttal to Hansen, he asserted that only this problem
indicated any "fundamental change" in the cyclical process.[88] Surely the great surge of consumer durables
purchase might have possessed the very self-reversing
propensities that Schumpeter sought in the expansion of
the 1920's. Yet Schumpeter--remarkably like Hansen--
veered away from this solution even as he sketched in
its outlines. To some extent at least, then, the interpretative stance of both men remained ambivalent.
Despite the thematic economy of both writers, they
seemed guilty of a sort of over-explanation. They saw
the prominence of consumer durables as a substantive
issue, yet they elaborated whole systems of interpretation which functioned irrespective of this new factor.

Schumpeter and Hansen purported to be in flatt-
est contradiction, particularly on the matter of
investment opportunities. Yet both wrote to cluminate
the technological interpretation of economic history.
Both gave partial, and diminishing, emphasis to the
institutionally fostered problem of high costs. Both
showed greatly dampened interest in the international

---

[88]Schumpeter, Cycles, v. 2, 1037.

financial origins of the American crisis. Both tied the
initial severity of the Depression, in part, to the
large role of consumer durables in the prior boom.
When it came to the current misfortunes of the economy,
their areas of accord seemed forsaken. The middle
thirties had brought about a full scale division among
investment-oriented economists. But the American
environment provided a continuing basis for mediation
between Hansen's Keynesianism and Schumpeter's evolved
neo-orthodoxy.

CHAPTER VI

STAND-OFF IN THE DEBATE OVER STAGNATION;
MEDIATING APPROACHES DEVELOP FURTHER

The great works of Hansen and Schumpeter in
1938-39 marked an end as well as a beginning. They
were the initial, monumental thesis and antithesis of
the American controversy over secular stagnation.
Almost by the same token, they brought to a conclusion
the period in which interpretation of the specific con-
tours of the 1920's and 1930's seemed a primary task of
economics. Indeed, in the aftermath of the collapse of
1937-1938, pragmatic issues were already taking preced-
ence. The collapse entirely vindicated the spirit of
Keynes' General Theory: doctrinaire elaboration of the
causes of chronic underemployment seemed less urgent
than consideration of remedial courses of action.
Hansen's arguments represented the most radical historical proofs of the need for government intervention, and
so they received continuing attention through the war
period and even afterward. But a narrowing atmosphere
of polemics inevitably came to surround these

proceedings, including even Hansen's reiteration of his
thesis. Schumpeter, having completed his detailed historical exposition, moved on to flesh out the sociology
of the future demise of capitalism.[1] Approaches to
synthetic modes of interpretation, in the Clarkian
manner, so clearly broached by both Schumpeter and
Hansen, now seemed less imminent than before. Mediating
tendencies were in fact making progress, but in a rather
inexplicit and complicated fashion.

The debate over economic policy after the recession of 1937-38 naturally centered on government spending.
Many economists agreed with Hansen that the return of
Roosevelt's administration to the policy of budget
balancing had been instrumental in renewing depression.
Schumpeter expressed great annoyance at the extent of
economists' agreement that government spending had
played a key role in economic movements from 1933 to
1938.[2] In any case, there was after 1938 lively

_____

[1]We have not time to discuss <u>Capitalism, Socialism, and Democracy</u> (1942). One ought to say that its
methodology embodied the grandest exercise in institutionalist economic history accomplished in America since
Veblen. That a relatively orthodox figure like
Schumpeter had so fully appropriated institutionalism,
was another illustration of that discipline's inherent
neutrality in economics. Anyway, the unification of the
orientation toward equilibrium economics and institutionalism was consummated, after forty years of rivalry.

[2]Schumpeter, <u>Business Cycles</u> (New York, 1939),
v. 2, 1005, 1014.

controversy as to the potential benefits of augmented government spending. Many economists considered that the lesson of the American 1930's had been not that more spending was required, but that spending policies simply were not conducive to the rehabilitation of investment.[3] J. M. Clark, for one, in an article of 1939, argued that temporary "pump-priming" had failed to overcome the cautiousness of investors in the 1930's: they had anticipated its early cessation. On the other hand, he held that fuller, long-term spending plans would be viewed by business as disquieting forerunners of higher taxation, inflation, or impairment of public credit.[4] Clark considered that the theory of secular investment stagnation remained unproven, although it was clear that investment needed some kind of encouragement. He suggested that some forms of income redistribution were in order to maintain consumer demand--but laid down that policies as threatening to business as increased corporate taxation or government spending ought to be avoided.[5]

---

[3]For example, cf. John Williams, "Deficit Spending," American Economic Review, v. 30, February 1941, 52-66.

[4]J. M. Clark, "Compensatory Devices," reprinted in Readings in Business Cycle Theory, American Economic Association (Philadelphia, 1944), 299-313. (Originally in American Economic Review, March, 1939.)

[5]Ibid., 308-310.

It is not necessary for our purposes fully to
sample the writings that comprised the debate over
government spending. Its nature, and its urgency, are
perhaps suggested by the difficulties it had raised for
Clark. In 1934, and still in 1939, Clark personally
favored deep structural intervention into the activities
of all durables industries. But he clearly feared the
relatively superficial public interference entailed by
spending policies. Clark, like many economists, had
found harrowing the protracted partial participation of
the government in the economy of the 1930's.[6] Anxiety
over what had been done by government, joining
Schumpeter's more refined fear of what had been
threatened, inevitably founded an entire school of
interpretation of the Depression. This viewpoint, often
buttressed by the critique of rigid costs (as in Mills),
represented the most dogged antagonist of the Keynes-
Hansen concept of inherent investment stagnation.

---

[6]Clark's revised and expanded edition of the
large work of 1926 appeared in 1939 (Social Control of
Business (Chicago, 1939). His Preface stated clearly
the need for systematic control of the economy, or,
minimally, control at "strategic points." He urged "not
piecemeal reforms, but . . . comprehensive treatment of
an organic malady, ramifying throughout the system."
His new chapter on the Depression and the questions it
had raised, was not unlike his views as of Strategic
Factors. The new work was less detailed, and less
designed to bring attention to the accelerator and consumer durables. It still incorporated them, in the
context of one of the most graceful short accounts of
the nature of the business cycle I have ever seen.
Cf. Social Control, 405-422.

The arguments on both sides were made, as never before, with reference to immediate issues of policy. In such an atmosphere, eclectic or mediating interpretative ventures were discouraged. The question which engrossed attention was--had investment been retarded by inherent lack of outlets or by external, institutional factors?

Clark's earlier synthesis of autonomous factors, appealing to properties of both investment and consumption, had grown out of a different sort of polarization of economic opinion. In 1932-34 institutional aggravations were stressed by both sides of the debate--the investment-oriented and the consumption-oriented. Clark had stood aloof from both, yet clearly mediated. In the late thirties the whole concept of autonomous causation lay on one side of the division of opinion. This concept in turn had been hurriedly bound to the characteristic problem of the thirties, that of investment. On the other side of the division lay the methodology of institutionalism, largely dissociated from its anti-business origins, and adapted for the explanation of the failure of investment. If consumer durables tended to have autonomous patterns of purchase, this merely was subsumed under the autonomous approach to investment. Hansen had construed the matter of consumer durables as an aspect of the overall problem of

investment outlets: new outlets for both investor and
consumer capital seemed lacking. Moreover, if the prosperity of the twenties had resulted from vast, interacting booms of business and consumer investment--such a
situation was conspicuous by its absence in the thirties.

And so Hansen and his opponents carried on the
debate without special concern over the matter of consumer durables or accelerator interaction. Hansen, in
his Presidential address to the American Economic Association in December of 1938, and in a chapter of his large
text <u>Fiscal Policy and Business Cycles</u> of 1941, made
almost identical statements of his thesis.[7] In both he
spoke inclusively of diminished outlets for "investment."
He emphasized declining population growth more than
before, and treated consequent decline in housing needs
as a key aspect of the investment problem. Distinctions
between consumers' and investors' capital apparently
seemed unnecessary to him now. In any case, he held
that population growth had always been a major basis not
only for housing construction but also for all forms of
investment. He estimated that in the past population
growth had induced roughly one half of all capital

_____

[7]Alvin Hansen, "Economic Progress and Declining
Population Growth," in <u>Readings in Business Cycle Theory</u>,
American Economic Association (1944), 367-383. (Origin-
ally in <u>American Economic Review</u>, March 1939.)

formation in Europe and America. Closely bound to population growth had been the development of promising new
territories; now both processes seemed to have consider-
ably slowed. The growth of America had provided an out-
let for European capital, but now that America had
matured no such land of opportunity had appeared to
replace her.

The other basis for progress in investment,
besides the "extensive" stimuli of demographic and
territorial development, lay in the "intensive" uses of
capital. These had been fostered as technology had made
possible the replacement of labor by producers' capital.
Here too, as he had before, Hansen feared that new conditions were taking effect. He argued that available
statistics indicated that over the last fifty years, at
least in many industries, the ratio of capital to its
output of goods was no longer rising. (That is, labor-
saving innovations were also capital-saving, and allowed
increased output without increased capital investment.)
To be sure, Hansen seemed less certain than he had in
Full Recovery that this trend was affecting industry at
large and on the average. And so he returned at this
juncture, in both the statements under consideration, to
the problem of housing.[8] Housing, though based on

---

[8]Hansen, "Economic Progress," 375-376; Fiscal
Policy and Business Cycles (New York, 1941), 357-358.

"extensive" growth, embodied highly "intensive" use of
capital: hence, in the American 1920's housing had
accounted for one quarter of total net capital formation. If population and housing ceased to grow, this in
itself would effect a basic trend away from intensive
outlets for capital. Hansen summarized the outlook for
intensive investment as follows: it seemed unencouraging in industry overall, and certainly grim in housing.

For the rest, Hansen asserted that whatever the
trends in extensive or intensive uses of capital, real
prosperity could only be maintained by the rise of whole
new industries. No industry commensurate with the auto
industry had been available for basic development in the
1930's, and was not in any way guaranteed for the next
decade. Furthermore--and here Hansen invoked accelerator
theory--stabilization of production of recently expanded
industries, even at high levels, was not sufficient to
maintain prosperity. Hansen urged, though without
elaboration, that it was precisely in the development
of great individual industries that the accelerator
principle operated with peculiar power, first to stimulate general prosperity and then to undermine it.[9]
Hansen did not specifically discuss the cycle of 1921-33:

---

[9]Hansen, "Economic Progress," 379; Fiscal Policy,
362.

he was speaking generally of the unlikelihood that
current stagnation could be overcome without forceful
aid from great new industries. He added that even if
such latter should arise, the decline of population
growth and territorial expansion would promise difficulties in the future of investment.[10] Finally, he
adverted in 1938 and 1941 to the complicating matters of
"monopolistic" rigidities in both wages and prices.
These questions he still considered as important, but
subordinate, problems affecting the outlook for investment.[11]

Hansen's work had not greatly evolved since
Full Recovery. It was mainly more compactly and self-
assuredly devoted to the contention that contemporary
investment faced a dearth of outlets. And the most
influential criticisms of Hansen took up matters quite
precisely in his terms. The most exhaustive critique
was that of George Terborgh, The Bogey of Economic
Maturity, published in 1945. Terborgh was a business
economist rather than an academic, and his work was
sponsored by a business foundation. In any event,
Terborgh's book provoked an exchange of articles between

---

[10]Hansen, Fiscal Policy, 364.

[11]Hansen, "Economic Progress," 380-381; Fiscal
Policy, 363.

Hansen, himself, and others in 1946. When this was done,
there seemed to exist a growing sense of stalemate on a
number of questions. On the important issue of population growth, Terborgh argued from statistics persuasively.
He emphasized that the percentage rate of increase of
population in America had been in gradual decline since
1850. Thus the economy must have been undergoing
constant adjustment to this trend, and should not have
suddenly collapsed in the later phases of the adjustment.[12]
Hansen rejoined that nonetheless the fact that population
growth first began to slacken in absolute terms during
the mid-1920's, did set the stage for ensuing difficulties in investment.[13] As to the effects of frontier
expansion on investment, Terborgh pointed out that
capital formation had been slightly higher as a proportion of national product from 1900 to 1930 than it had
been earlier; and that overall prosperity had been more
marked in the more mature period.[14] Hansen answered
sharply that the economic development of the newer
states had been a major theme in American advance at
least until World War I.[15]

[12]George Terborgh, The Bogey of Economic Maturity (Chicago, 1945), 48-49.

[13]Hansen, "Notes on Terborgh," Review of
Economic Statistics, v. 28, February 1946, 14.

[14]Terborgh, Bogey, 65.

[15]Hansen, "Notes on Terborgh," 15.

On the matter of the vital role of great new
industries, Terborgh stressed that the railroads in their
heyday accounted for no more than 15% of all capital
formation, autos and subordinate industries during the
1920's no more than 20%. He went on to urge that older
industries, while suffering a decline in their rate of
growth, have ordinarily absorbed increasing absolute
amounts of investment. Old industries did not die, but
underwent continual technological evolution. If net
new investment tapered off, replacement needs steadily
grew. Terborgh cited the example of autos: by the end
of the 1920's consumer replacement of autos represented
over two-thirds of output, more than offsetting the
slackening growth of total cars in use.[16] Hansen
accepted Terborgh's figures. Yet he was satisfied that
new industries which contributed 15 to 20% of overall
investment had in fact made the difference between prosperity and stagnation. He charged that Terborgh had
simply overlooked the great expansionary "multiplier-
accelerator" leverage of such industrial episodes.[17]
Terborgh in turn replied that he had perfect faith in
"multiplier-accelerator" effects, but saw no reason why
they might not be derived over a broad front, from

---

[16]Terborgh, Bogey, 78-90.

[17]Hansen, "Notes on Terborgh," 15.

precisely the sort of general innovative activity that
had characterized the 1920's.[18]

Terborgh made myriad arguments under each of
these and other headings. But it may be seen that in
basic approach, he carried on the intelligent New Era
tradition of Mitchell in 1929 and of Schumpeter in 1939.
At one point he reminded the reader that Mitchell and
other economists of the 1920's had greeted reduced
population growth as the harbinger of increased per
capita wealth. This construction seemed to him ultimately no less wise than Hansen's.[19] For his most
general conception was that symptoms of economic maturity had been long developing in America without reversing expansionary tendencies. Just as Schumpeter had,
Terborgh let interpretative questions stand or fall on
the matter of the 1920's. He held that investment-
stagnationism was at its worst in explaining the abrupt
transition to Depression which took place in 1929-1933.
He maintained at the outset that the "rich and varied
technological progress" of the 1920's simply could not

[18]Terborgh, "Dr. Hansen on The Bogey of
Economic Maturity," Review of Economic Statistics, v.
28, August 1946, 171.

[19]Terborgh, Bogey, 45-46. Indeed, the trend
toward higher per capita production in America was
fairly well borne out by the important N.B.E.R. study of
Arthur F. Burns, Production Trends in the United States
Since 1870 (New York, 1934); cf. 279-80.

have come so suddenly to an impasse.[20] Terborgh turned
with particular vengeance on Hansen's characterization of
the prosperity of the 1920's as due to a confluence of
superficial causes. Hansen, as we have seen, had viewed
the twenties as a time of developing dearth of outlets
to traditional investment, shored up by foreign lending,
postwar housing shortage, installment purchases of automobiles and so forth. Terborgh held, precisely in
Schumpeter's vein, that the entire period had been a
typical cyclical experience comparable to many earlier
ones.[21] If investment had failed at its culmination, so
had consumption--due to the incursions of the stock
market crash. He added that the behavior of consumers
in withholding purchases of durables had operated in the
contraction just as had the inhibition of investors.[22]
Terborgh pressed the question: if a cyclical contraction of the auto, housing, and other industries had
taken place, how did this indicate a new condition of
restricted outlets for investment?[23]

---

[20]Terborgh, Bogey, 174, 188.

[21]Ibid., 176.

[22]Ibid., 184-186.

[23]Ibid., 188-189.

In his reply, Hansen rephrased his explanation of
the conditions of the 1920's. Writing succinctly, he
mentioned the peak population growth of the mid-twenties
(in absolute terms), and the broad-based advances of the
automobile and electrical industries. He also contended
that there was nothing in his earlier writings which con-
flicted with a largely cyclical view of the onset of
Depression; he especially protested agreement with
Terborgh as to the incidence of a partly normal cycle
in housing construction.[24] In short, it began to be
evident that much of the dialogue involved fairly tenuous
distinctions. Perhaps the outstanding areas of confusion
were the following: first, Hansen's unconvincing effort
to maintain that the prosperity of the twenties had been
largely unsound (a position from which he finally
appeared to back away). Second, there was Terborgh's
unwillingness to perceive anything essential to the
1920's which militated toward catastrophe. Terborgh
discussed the afflictions of the thirties as quite
separate from prior economic currents. (He mentioned as
causes of retarded recovery the abnormal rise of building
costs, and the discouragements of the external political
environment.) [25] His aim was consistently to promote the

---

[24]Hansen, "Notes on Terborgh," 16.

[25]Terborgh, Bogey, 178-181..

view that the prior cycle had been a precedented experi-
ence--and, more particularly, that it did not indicate
any new categorical infirmity of investment.

All in all, it may be that the great debate had
lost more in clarity than it had gained since
Schumpeter's work of 1939. Yet resolution of the
debate seemed in some ways further off. Nonetheless,
there was evidence of an entering wedge of compromise.
Certain analytical developments during the war years may
have contributed to Terborgh's idea--and to Hansen's
partial admission--that an ordinary cycle in housing had
been at issue in 1921-33. Increasing interest was
attaching to the concept of a quasi-autonomous building
cycle, as a key to the problem of the relative intensity
of different business cycles. When Hansen, in Full
Recovery, had dilated on the relation of population
trends to the housing industry, he had referred to a
study by William Newman of 1935. Newman's emphasis,
taken up by Hansen, had been upon the role of urban
population growth in regulating the building cycle.[26]
Rather different emphases obtained in Clarence Long's
Building Cycles of 1940, which quickly became a major
authority. Long's chief aim was to demonstrate an

---

[26]William H. Newman, The Building Industry and
Business Cycles (Chicago, 1935). Cf. Hansen, Full
Recovery, 299.

inherent and profound cyclicality in construction. Discussing all types of construction together, industrial and residential, Long called them the largest single "investment goods industry."[27] And Long showed from statistical history that the cyclical fluctuations of construction were the widest of any important industry.[28] Finally, building had tended to lead the economy into its cyclical contractions (particularly in the severe depressions of the 1870's, 1890's, and 1930's)--and to be slow in recovering. Long did not discuss population trends much: his approach was to consider building as the most inherently volatile element in the investment cycle.

His explanation of this volatility was largely based on the relative durability of construction. Buildings, whether factories or homes, were so long-lived that they were in Long's view investment goods <u>par excellance</u>. Hence he argued that their production was more sensitively attuned to the general business outlook than any other products; and he made a case for the correlation of building cycles with the history of conditions in the securities markets (taking these as an

[27]Clarence D. Long, Jr., <u>Building Cycles</u> (Princeton, 1940), 5.

[28]Long, <u>Building Cycles</u>, 9, 155-156.

indicator of business expectations). Long emphasized
that it was the durability of the investment that caused
this sensitivity--and the related factor that building
often was undertaken to replace older existing units.
These latter were normally durable and still usable, so
that new structures were highly postponable.[29] In all
this, Long was very reminiscent of Clark and his stress
on consumer and producer durables. Nor did Long hesitate to make a general assertion that durability of
product was the key to the severity of the Depression.
He pointed out that durable goods had risen from 31% of
industrial output in 1879 to 44% in 1929; and that output
of durables had fallen 85% in 1929-33, while non-durables
fell only 42%. Long made so bold as to conjecture that
if it were not for the volatile durables, the "relatively stable" other industries would be virtually
"absolutely stable."[30] Thus Long extrapolated from the
position of the Mills-Rorty-Clark school of 1932-34,
carrying that earlier emphasis as far as it could go.

Long's effort was not, however, directed toward
general interpretative ends. He was trying mainly to
establish the building cycle as the most unstable
element in the business cycle. The very elusive question

---

[29]Ibid., 93-94, 110-113, 192, 209.

[30]Ibid., 3, 4.

of whether construction more largely initiated great
cyclical movements or reflected and intensified them,
Long did not attempt to solve. He did clearly consider
that construction, taken together with the other durables,
both initiated and intensified cycles. Since construction was the most durable and postponable of all goods,
Long seemed to incline to the idea that construction,
moving with business expectations, played a peculiarly
intensifying role. Yet perhaps construction was often
the first major industry to convert slightly reduced
expectations into actual decrease of output. In any
event, whatever the distinctions which remained to be
pondered, Long's work left the impression that the building cycle functioned with quasi-autonomous cyclicality.
His views could not disqualify the Newman-Hansen notion
of heavy dependence of construction on demographic
trends. But Long had surely contributed to the view
that the recent Collapse had to do with increased cyclical propensities rather than with diminished opportunities. The construction cycle of course was nothing new;
but perhaps, in league with other advancing durables, it
found a new extremity.

Yet Long's book, and other signs of increased
scrutiny of the building cycle, worked to fortify the
trend toward analytic concentration upon autonomous

patterns of investment, divorced from consumption. Clark
had discussed consumer durables, with natural emphasis on
the two great products, housing and autos. The new
orientation to the building cycle firmly coupled residential construction with commercial and industrial,
under the category of investment.[31] This was perfectly
logical, since all forms of construction, as Long put it,
represented the longest-term sort of investment.
Further, all used credit liberally; and residential
construction was usually done by business contractors in
advance of actual orders from consumers.[32] In any case,
consideration of construction as an aspect of the traditional investment cycle, a practice which inevitably
became more established, left consumer durables a category of diminished interest. Though Long had not really
intended this, the trend toward focus on autonomous
investment was strengthened (and hence perhaps Hansen's
investment stagnationism as well).

This trend reached a brilliant synthetic culmination in an article of 1942 by Walter Isard, "Transport

---

[31]Treatment of the building cycle as an entity
was certainly not new; Long's work was simply a major
step in rededication to the field. For an earlier
example of writing on building as quasi-autonomous,
see John Riggleman, "Building Cycles in the U. S. 1875-
1932," American Statistical Association, v. 28, June
1933.
[32]Long, Building Cycles, 190, 200.

Development and Building Cycles." Isard was to receive his doctorate in 1943, and to teach regional and locational economics at M.I.T. and the University of Pennsylvania, where he was a professor of economics after 1956. Isard's work of 1942 brought technological history and business cycles into a deeper and more unambiguous fusion than even Schumpeter had achieved. The basis of the fusion was a simple juxtaposition of the statistical histories of the growth of transport facilities and the building cycle. In a single chart, Isard showed a remarkable correlation in the two series. His interpretation was that great advances in transportation had, over the past century, created the basis for synchronous waves of construction in the areas newly thrown open. He argued straightforwardly that the transport had "caused" the building. In cycles where building seemed to precede transport, Isard held that speculative building had occurred in anticipation of expected transport facilities.[33] These events, dominating the major movements of the American economy, had produced their effects quite apart from specific trends in population growth.[34]

---

[33] Walter Isard, "Transport Development and Building Cycles," Quarterly Journal of Economics, v. 57, November 1942, 93, 106.

[34] Ibid., 111.

Isard's chart showed first the great boom in canal building (1825-35) with its construction cycle running a few years behind. Then came the several waves of railroad installation, each with its building boom. From 1889 to 1905 Isard argued that a waning building boom had been shored up, then carried to new heights, by the surge of municipal tramway investment. This building boom went on till the War, reinforced by the automobile after 1910. While the tram had widened the cities, the auto had thrown open the entire suburbs for construction. The sharpest increase in auto registrations, just before the War and in the early 1920's, had slightly preceded and set the stage for the bulk of the building boom of the twenties.[35] In each great episode, Isard held, both the transport and the dependent building cycle had represented large speculative investment, proceeding irrespective of initial profit conditions and timed only by the innovations in transport. That often the later stages of the building boom had given way to protracted depression of construction, Isard attributed to frantic overbuilding ahead of actual demand. For revival, under these conditions, building had to await the next major development in transportation. Such was

---

[35]*Ibid.*, 100-106.

the situation in the 1930's. And Isard predicted that after the War advances in air transport, and a related building boom, might easily dispel stagnation.[36]

Isard was in accord with the basic method of Schumpeter and Hansen, construing autonomous investment in innovations as the prime economic mover. His focus on transport did not necessarily preclude attention to other great industries, such as the electrical and chemical after 1900. And he had bound the movements of construction into patterns of autonomous investment more than had ever been attempted. Although he did not pursue the stagnationist possibilities of his system, they were great. Should there be no major advances of transport after the War (though further extension of autos and roads ought to have been an important possibility under his theory), then Isard would have to gird himself for stagnation in building and probably in general. Not only had Isard ignored movements of consumer demand (for example purchases of housing qua consumption), he made no mention of income-stimulating effects of investment, or reflex accelerator effects. Schumpeter, while focusing on investment, had viewed the housing boom of the 1920's as largely a function of the consumer prosperity

---

[36]Ibid., 111.

generated so amply in the period.[37] Schumpeter had in
fact also remarked that the auto boom and the suburban
housing boom were importantly related.[38] But he had not
really approximated Isard's imposing skeletal version of
the cycle of the twenties, picturing autos and construction as the unitary backbone of the giant.

Isard's dogmatic integration of the building and
transport cycles never achieved more than partial
acceptance by economists. His work complemented current
interpretative trends most clearly where it emphasized
the autonomous force of the building cycle (irrespective
of its enabling conditions in transport). Isard and
Long were in rough agreement that building cycles
attained a momentum of their own, and in their contraction phases, had played an important aggravating role in
the three largest recent depressions (those of the 1870's,
1890's, and 1930's). Both writers included simple over-
building in their explanation of the upper turning point
in the building cycle. Prior over-building and subsequent decline in construction, of course, had from an
early date been described as an important element in the
severity of the Depression. Mitchell's article of 1933,
for example, had included this line of thought, while

[37]Schumpeter, Business Cycles, v. 2, 744.
[38]Ibid., 754.

describing broader conditions of over-investment and speculation.[39] But now the notion of a special and semi-independent cyclicality in building was gaining prominence, providing a basis for a new view of cyclical history as a whole. Long described the ordinary building cycle as requiring 13-23 years to run its course; it was longer than the (roughly 10 year) cycle in general business. The length of the building cycle Long considered related to the durability of building--that is, slow depreciation set the stage only for occasional cycles of replacement.[40] This, of course, did not account for the great length of the expansion phase of the building cycle, or the high volume of construction accomplished over a given cycle. These doubtless were based simply upon the vast need of society for construction. As to varying lengths and intensities of individual building cycles, several factors seemed important: population growth, transport advance, and the general level of economic activity.

Whether or not one of the above factors was dominant in differentiating building cycles, they were inherently sharp and self-reversing. Hence Terborgh did

---

[39]See above, p. 51.

[40]Long, Building Cycles, 163.

have a partly valid objection to stagnationism on the
basis that general contraction (1929-33) had been
accentuated by the coincidence of a "normal" cyclical
downswing of construction. And Hansen was forced to
moderate his stress on declining population growth as
the key to stagnation in construction in the Depression.
Naturally, the debate over broader stagnation of investment outlets was not resolved; but it was, potentially,
somewhat tamed. A full example of a modified version of
Hansen's interpretation was provided by a study of 1942
by an English economist, Thomas Wilson. This work, a
fine and detailed analysis of the American 1920's and
1930's, has remained one of the most influential treat-
ments of the period. Wilson held that the Collapse was
due partly to exhaustion of investment outlets, and perhaps more so to saturation of demand for construction.[41]
Wilson described residential housing as a particularly
crucial factor: reaching a peak of $5.2 billion in 1925,
it fell to $4.3 in 1928 and to only $3 billion in 1929.
He argued convincingly that neither construction costs
nor credit supply could explain the decline, but only
the conditions of supply and demand for housing (he
pointed to the decline in rents beginning in 1925 as

[41]Thomas Wilson, Fluctuations in Income and
Employment (London, 1942), 156.

evidence of general oversupply). Wilson did not attempt further to explain the downswing in demand for housing; it was simply a fact, which, when joined by the overall contraction of the economy, helped bring on vast deflation.[42] Wilson went on to stress the continued weakness of residential construction (still 30% below 1929 levels in 1937) as in large measure responsible for the incompleteness of general recovery.[43]

Wilson, in the end, gravitated more to Keynes' formulation of the 1920's and 1930's than to Hansen's. He saw the 1920's as a period of unusual proliferation of capital goods, with the stock of buildings the "most striking example."[44] He did treat suggestively the reduced role of great innovations, and the retarded advance of productivity during the thirties. (This latter emphasis already represented a revision of Hansen, who had feared that increased productivity might be attained at the expense of the volume of investment.) But he viewed the twenties as having accomplished a surge of investment—not only in construction but in equipment—which was not likely to be sustained, simply

[42]Ibid., 156-157.

[43]Ibid., 183.

[44]Ibid., 186.

on the face of it. Given this, Wilson's idea of the
thirties seemed not to require any "stagnation" of outlets, but only a relatively less exciting set of
advances, to interpret declension from the prior heights.
Inevitably, such a moderated stagnationism would prove
durable in economic literature, and fortify the new tradition of explicit orientation to Keynes' General Theory.
But it had been, above all, the increased attention to
the statistics and concept of the building cycle which
told, and provided grounds for partial mediation of the
debate ever secular stagnation. Keynes, of course, had
conceived some sort of stagnation as the plight of
nations possessing a great capital stock. By now, in
the 1940's, there were signs that the problem might
better be understood as one of heightened cyclicality.

Accelerator theory still embodied one of the
most powerful tools of business cycle theory. And while
economists were increasingly preoccupied with the
history and conditions of autonomous investment, the
accelerator interaction continued to fuel discussion and
controversy. Hansen, as we have seen, gave the accelerator a place in describing the transition of great
industries to maturity. Accelerator theory, however,
received its most thorough treatment in the developing
field of formal business cycle theory. Precise mathematical models of the cycle were more and more under

construction, particularly after Keynes established the importance of a roughly quantifiable investment "multiplier." This gave most direct encouragement to efforts to calculate the effects of increments in government spending upon income. A concrete formulation for such purposes, combining the multiplier and the accelerator, was contributed by Paul Samuelson of M.I.T. in 1939.[45] In the effort to develop multiplier-accelerator models of the business cycle as a whole, R. F. Harrod and other English theorists continued to lead the way. Harrod further developed his ideas of 1936, in an essay of 1939 which was to gain increasing influence. There Harrod emphasized the general dependence of investment upon the rate of increase of income, rather than autonomous factors.[46] Harrod's road was uphill; but by 1950 important support was forthcoming from John Hicks, also of Oxford. Hicks' book on business cycles of that year was, for a time, perhaps the most respected authority in its field. Like Harrod, Hicks argued that rendering

----

[45] Paul Samuelson, "Interactions Between the Multiplier Analysis and the Principle of Acceleration," Review of Economic Statistics, v. 21, May 1939, 75-78.

[46] R. F. Harrod, "An Essay in Dynamic Theory," in Readings in Business Cycles and National Income, Alvin Hansen ed., (New York, 1953), 200-219. (Originally in Economic Journal, v. 49, March 1939.)

Keynesian analysis truly dynamic--so as to embrace the business cycle as a whole--required the accelerator orientation.[47] There is no need to discuss here the various controversies which arose over modes of incorporating the accelerator into formal models. The rough point is sufficient: while economic interpretation of the 1930's focused on intrinsic tendencies in investment, abstract cycle analysis was coming to rely on the dynamic interaction between investment and consumption.

In normal interpretative usage, the study of the building cycle was reinforcing the trend toward viewing the larger business cycle as based upon autonomous movements of investment. Yet the highly cyclical properties of building seemed to suggest the presence of the amplifying and reversing qualities more readily connected with "induced" investment (generated according to accelerator principle, from general prosperity). Long's emphasis on the durability of construction, and on its resultant responsiveness to extraneous influences, allowed the building cycle a dependent quality. The replacement cycle in construction was physically given by the longevity of buildings: yet replacement was

---

[47]John R. Hicks, A Contribution to the Theory of the Trade Cycle (Oxford, 1961), 1-8. (Original Preface of 1949, reprinted).

precisely the most postponable element of investment. To
a surprising extent, the question as to whether construction demand moved according to absolute needs or to relative conditions, was open to debate. It was by relativ-
ity and trend that the accelerator principle functioned.
The older Clarkian view of the special accelerator interaction of the 1920's, deriving from patterns of consumer
and producer durable consumption, still held interpretative possibilities. Perhaps it was not mere coincidence
that the building cycle and the general business cycle
had been so dangerously synchronized in 1921-33.
Certainly Isard had made a case for related auto and
construction booms as integral to the prosperity of the
period. And if those booms reinforced one another in
terms of social and technological development, surely
they worked together to launch a very intense expansion
in terms of (multiplier-accelerator) income stimulation.
Moreover, perchance Isard was right that the very heart
of autonomous investment always lay in the transport
area. Then in the twenties, for the first time, (because
autos were the transport innovation) this investment was
after all not autonomous, but closely attuned to current
consumer demand. Picturing things in this way, we should
consider the twenties a vast boom in induced investment,
having in the end no autonomous, long-term investment
basis, and hence yielding to an unprecedented

contractionary accelerator effect.

Of course the above view of the 1920's, like the strictly investment-based views, is concerned with great autonomous movements, and not institutional conditions. Focus on the latter, by the end of the war if nct sooner, seemed in full decline. The orthodox critique of wage rigidity and reckless government policies (from the New Era to the New Deal) still gained expression. So too did the general critique of rigidities, and the special liberal case against underconsumptionist effects of rigidity.[48] But Samuelson summarized the situation fairly in 1943: the idea that rigidity was the key to economic difficulties would have to be considered an "extreme" view.[49] Samuelson freely asserted that Keynesian criteria upheld the desirability of flexible prices and costs. But he considered the crux of the economic problem to be maintenance of high levels of investment. Samuelson did not bother to analyze long-run

---

[48]Seymour E. Harris, ed., _Postwar Economic Problems_ (New York, 1943); for orthodox views see Schumpeter and Slichter essays. A strong statement of liberal price critique is the John Williams essay in _Financing American Prosperity_, The Twentieth Century Fund (New York, 1945).

[49]Samuelson, "Full Employment After the War," in Harris ed., _Postwar Economic Problems_, 39.

stagnationist possibilities; he simply urged that it
would be too risky to end wartime taxation. Laconically,
he anticipated the course of least resistance which would
prevail in postwar America. He ruminated that continued
high levels of government spending might sufficiently
shore up investment, without resort to budget deficits.[50]

The tendency of economic thought, interpretative
and policy-oriented, may be considered to have entered a
phase of urgent focus in 1937 to 1945. Investment
comprised the underpinning of the capitalist order, and
investment had repeated its failure of 1929-33 as early
as 1937. Whatever the precise reasons, investment could
fairly be viewed as having lost its autonomous force.
Whether this foundation had rotted of itself, or been
shaken by modern political and institutional evolution,
was not subject to real verification. The broadest road
to a workable compromise seemed to lay in the comparison
of the 1930's to past cyclical tribulations of investment. From Schumpeter to Terborgh, the opponents of
secular stagnationism partly gravitated in this direction
even while delineating the influence of recent institutional developments. Hansen, while he feared longer-
term difficulties, had from the outset carefully based

[50]Ibid., 27-44.

his characterizations on historical precedent, appealing particularly to Spiethoff's views of the depressed 1890's. By 1942, when Isard's study was published, a context for the discussion of the cyclical history of investment had been fully suggested. Thus the stage was set for the mitigation of controversy over the wider questions of stagnation, even while the controversy ran on. Laying bare the checkered history of investment, especially the cycles of construction activity, provided a kind of solution: the experience of 1920-1940 embodied just another great cycle of (autonomous) investment, like others only greater. As to policy, this notion was sufficient to show the way in the clearest terms: if investment were too low, it should be supplemented by government spending.

Keeping matters as simple as possible, the reason for the extremity of this cyclical depression of investment might be found in the enormity of prior accumulation of durable capital. This was Keynes' basic idea of the events in America, and Wilson had provided further support for that idea. Newly established opinion on the workings of the cycle in construction roughly corroborated this view of overactivity followed by a lull. In fact, even Long's effort (in the vein of Mills-Rorty-Clark) to discover a new exaggeration in the business cycle due to greater durability of products--could be seen as directly contributing to the Keynesian interpretation. Keynes' view had represented no real advance over Mitchell's (overinvestment) idea as of 1933, or the concepts of early investment-oriented cycle theory. With emphasis on the trend to durability, especially in consumers' goods (viewed here as forms of investment), the intensity of investment during the 1920's received explanation. Without that added emphasis, of course, the Keynes-Wilson attitude seemed rather spare and parochially English, and raised as many questions as it answered.

The haziness of Keynes' approach to business cycles was dealt with in a widely noted article of 1947 by Evsey Domar.[51] Domar held first that Keynes' fundamental short-term analysis of income determination was incomplete, because it did not incorporate fully the level of capital stock obtaining at a given time. On the other hand, in his treatment of the cycle as a whole, Keynes had placed heavy reliance on the role of expanded capital stock, in bringing on the curtailment of new investment. Domar urged that here Keynes had overlooked the implications of his own multiplier concept. (That

---

[51] Domar received his Ph.D. at Harvard in 1947, and has been a professor of economics at M.I.T. after 1957. He has been a major theorist of growth and cycles.

is, if investment had been high, it should have raised income and hence continually raised the marginal efficiency of further investment.) Domar held that the truth, in fact, lay somewhere between the two poles of Keynes' view.[52] His point was to indicate the extreme elusiveness of the problems of managing an economy so that the capital stock increased rapidly enough to buoy income, without bringing on conditions of overcapacity.[53] Domar's essay helped to launch highly intricate postwar analyses of the business cycle integrating the progress of the capital stock.

Domar did not specifically address the question of the collapse of the thirties. But his qualifications tended to show the insufficiency of an interpretation based solely on overexpansion of capital goods during the twenties. A powerful offset to the expansive multiplier effects on income seemed required to explain the terrible reversal of the whole trend of investment. A dearth of new outlets, added to the temporary saturation of the old, represented a possible such offset, and was implied by Keynes and elaborated by Hansen. But a major alternative construction was available in the view that an

---

[52]Evsey Domar, "Expansion and Employment," American Economic Review, v. 27, March 1947, 54.

[53]Ibid., 54.

intrinsically greater cyclicality prevailed, in which accelerator effects ran their course unimpeded. Such a view entailed that induced investment had come to a new predominance relative to autonomous investment--that investment had become more directly attuned to current consumption than previously. This view had the advantage that it explained the momentous reversal of investment without positing any discontinuity such as a sudden restriction of opportunities in the absolute sense. It might resolve the Keynesian paradox Domar described, in the manner of Clark: a mere slackening of expansion was adequate to bring absolute decline in investment. And, as Rorty and Clark had held, the resultant depression could proceed so far as to create a state of overcapacity in industry which ruled out invest-ment progress, quite irrespective of levels of opportun-ity (as judged by the standards sustained by the prior prosperity).

Generally, the way in which accelerator theory was absorbed into interpretation was as a minor theme, perhaps important in treatment of the turning point from prosperity to Depression. Since the turning point was a fundamental concern in business cycle theory per se, it is understandable that the accelerator was more impor-tant in that field than in general interpretation.

In any case, in either field the accelerator was not
considered an alternative to Keynesian assumptions, but
very much a complementary branch of Keynesian theory.
It had been viewed as an extension of multiplier analysis ever since Harrod had used it as such in 1936. The
accelerator took its place in evidence of the almost
infuriating breadth and flexibility of Keynesian
economics. With Keynes, while investment was the prime
mover, consumption supported and enhanced it, _via_ the
multiplier, over against savings. Distinction between
autonomous and induced investment were not subjects of
the General Theory, but were surely suggested by it.
In the postwar period such distinction was given firmer
attention by economists. For a short time, as will be
described, emphasis on induced investment and acceleration would appear to spill over from abstract cycle
theory into the interpretation of economic history _per_
_se_. But as the pattern of postwar stability emerged,
the needs of cycle analysis itself would rapidly shift.

For the time being, and again increasingly in
the recent postwar period, the most dynamic interpretative elements lay largely dormant, encompassed in the
broader Keynesian orientation. While Keynesians, down-
cast by the Depression, had developed an idea of investment outlets as absolutely restricted (so that a burst

of investment might overfill them), certain of their
analytic tools were fit to describe an almost wholly
relativistic view of the modern economy. The
Keynesians, of course, were prepared to seize upon these
tools--multiplier-accelerator concepts--to recreate a
prosperity which the given situation, the absolute
facts, had undermined. If they were somewhat dogged in
their interpretative orientation to autonomously generated investment, they were confessing their kinship to--
and yet more squarely confronting--the remnants of
classical economic tradition. These rested heavily on
the assumption that investment opportunities were not
only absolutely given, but, if not intemperately
tampered with by social ambition, almost absolutely
sufficient. Schumpeter best adapted these assumptions.
And the arduous debate over the status of unregulated
opportunity seemed a harsh enough collision between the
ancient principles of reformism and conservatism. Yet
Schumpeter had come far enough, in reconstructing
orthodox economics, toward a fully dynamic attitude--so
that even his work suggested the possibility of a middle
term in the debate. A middle term which lay on a
different plane, of course: for the idea of a cyclicality so powerful that it carried men from a maniacal
optimism to despair in three years, was an idea of a
world without fixed values.

CHAPTER VII

EPILOGUE AND CONCLUSION

The War and postwar periods have seen a large-
scale implementation of Keynesian programs of government
taxation and expenditure. The kind of social control
envisioned by the most ambitious economic observers of
this entire century has found its first great triumph.
Of course, structural reformers such as Tugwell have
been proven less prophetic than fiscal reformers such
as Foster and Catchings. Nonetheless, a partial culmination of the whole Progressive and Pragmatic tradition has been achieved--just as certainly as the New Era
has been reconstituted on a surer footing. Public power
has been used more trenchantly than the New Era synthe-
sizers led by Mitchell had projected; but capitalist
institutions are less changed than the Progressive and
institutionalist critics thought necessary. Most specifically, perhaps, the focal ambition of the New Era has
been realized, the stabilization of the business cycle.
Since, for thirty years, prosperity has not been sacrificed to this goal, it could well be said that even the
hoary heritage of classical equilibrium economics has

been vindicated, in a very general sense.

Such has been the quality of resolution and coming-together inherent in this postwar period. It has seemed for some time an almost Hegelian synthesis and transformation of prior tendencies and conflicts. (No doubt this sense of magic contributed greatly to indelible moral and practical errors such as the Vietnam involvement.) Just as there is no doubt that this period established an almost inscrutable brand of political liberal-conservatism, it should not be surprising that changed conditions importantly affected the economic disciplines which had been so instrumental in the change. First of all, economics completed, even abruptly, its evolution into a primarily practical endeavor. Concomitantly economic analysis became deeply preoccupied with contemporary matters. Keynes' General Theory had already embodied a trend toward intensive short-term analysis and the making of policy; now feats of historical description such as Hansen's and Schumpeter's would occupy a much less central place than they had in the economics of the 1930's. Business cycle analysis developed luxuriously and with ever more rigorous mathematical discipline. But the focus of the field had moved from interpretation of the past all the way to the forecasting of the future.

Inevitably, the economists' involvement with the contemporary economy influenced their views of the past, when they cared to consider it. There were, undoubtedly, both enhancements and distortions of perspective connected with the new situation. In any case, two rather opposed tendencies have been at work in recent interpretation of the interwar period. On the one hand, the simplifying method of construing past economic movements as a function of the flow of autonomous investment, has seemed less controversial than it was in Hansen's work of the 1930's. Yet on the other hand, there has been a clear revival of more eclectic or pluralistic ways of interpreting economic history. This latter tendency seems to predominate. Both tendencies are definitely fostered by the high and rising levels of government expenditure which have in the modern economy acted as a sustaining form of autonomous investment. By comparison, the wider business cycles of the past may readily be judged to have sprung from the relative fitfulness of basic investment. Yet the very fact that erratic economic impulses have been tamed, conduces to much greater attention to all the subtler disturbing factors in the economy. For example, concern with the functioning of financial mechanisms has come to be central to efforts to extend further control over the economy.

By the same token, interest in the financial elements of
the Collapse of 1929-33 has steadily grown, to the point
where it rivals its original high levels during these
harried years. Mitchell's eclectic but strongly financial
interpretation of 1933 makes more contemporary reading
now than it did in the middle thirties.[1]

In general economists reviewing the interwar era
have attempted both to set forth the basic trends in
autonomous investment, and to give weight to financial
and other imbalances which they consider to have importantly aggravated a necessarily deep Depression.
Accelerator theory, which we have considered a potential
mediating concept, has received diminishing attention in
interpretative works. This is prime evidence that
economists are concentrating on the methodologies consonant with a stabilized, rather than a dynamically
cyclical economy. John Hicks, who most persuasively

---

[1]In this context the large readership of
Galbraith's book of 1954, already a classic of a sort,
may be cited, and the more recently acclaimed work of
Milton Friedman; both, in their interpretations of the
severity of the Depression, rely heavily on the stock
market crash or other financial matters. Since neither
work can be considered fully representative of main-
stream thought in the economics profession, we will not
discuss them. Cf. John Kenneth Galbraith, The Great
Crash (Boston, 1954); and Milton Friedman and Anna J.
Schwartz, The Great Contraction (Princeton, 1963).
But for a more representative work in developed
mathematical form, with a large bias toward financial
factors, cf. Hyman Minsky, "A Linear Model of Cyclical
Growth" (1959), reprinted in Readings in Business Cycles
American Economic Association (Homewood, Ill., 1965).

postulated the role of acceleration in the business cycle, was under attack no sooner than he gained pre-eminence around 1950. Further, his own work of that time was already importantly concerned with methods of reining in the explosive effects of the accelerator principle in models of the business cycle. Hicks, and Harrod, considered that the stability of aggregate consumption ordinarily operated to prevent the downward accelerator interaction of investment and consumption from proceeding very far.[2] James Duesenberry of Harvard made a more pointed appeal to this matter in 1949, entitling it the "ratchet" effect. The argument was derived straightforwardly from the statistical fact that in depression consumption always declined less sharply than investment. Evidently there was a reluctance in consumers to suffer a decline in standards of living; hence, as their income fell they saved less, kept their consumption relatively high, and so put a floor under a contracting market.[3]

---

[2]John Hicks, A Contribution to the Theory of the Trade Cycle (Oxford, 1961), 31 (from original introduction of 1949, reprinted).

[3]James S. Duesenberry, Income, Saving, and the Theory of Consumer Behavior (Cambridge, 1949), 59-115.

These emphases came to represent a turning away from the accelerator aspects of depression. They did not, however, represent really new departures in economic analysis. Dominant schools of cycle theory had from the outset been oriented to the relative volatility of investment. As we have seen, the underconsumptionist school had been rather unsuccessfully wrestling with the sharper decline of investment than consumption since the facts became clear in the early thirties. Clark himself, in the course of elaborating the accelerator approach in 1934, had adduced the relative stability of consumption as a limiting factor. Investment declined because consumption stabilized late in the boom; investment ceased declining because consumption declined less readily.[4] That construction left plenty of room for a frightening enough Depression. The key question, thus, remained-- was investment sensitive enough to trends in consumption to create vast depressions out of stable situations; was investment primarily "induced" by consumption?

Such questions were still theoretically open. In one respect, Hicks indicated that acceleration might be more important than he had supposed in 1950. In a preface to the 1955 edition of his Trade Cycles, Hicks

---

[4]Clark, Strategic Factors, 79-89.

pondered whether he might have given autonomous investment too large a place in his model. He speculated
that a substantial portion of the investment he had
considered "autonomous" might be dependent on the long-
term trend of growth in an economy. Such investment,
while providing a floor in a minor depression, might be
postponed when serious contraction called in question
the larger growth trend.[5] The distinction between
autonomous and induced investment was necessarily vague;
the introduction of an intermediate term served further
to highlight the theoretical dilemma.

Concrete interpretation of the Depression, in
any case, went on with decreasing reference to any such
dilemma. The best example of interpretative trends is
fortunately provided by the works of the economist who
has done the most important and detailed interpretation
during the postwar period. This is Professor R. A.
Gordon of Berkeley. In his first contribution, a long
essay of 1950, Gordon was firmly oriented to the
technicological approach of Schumpeter and Hansen, and
at the same time to the accelerator concept. After care-
ful analysis of the 1920's, Gordon concluded that they
were a time of rare flowering of investment opportunities. Partial exhaustion of these outlets he

---

[5]Hicks, Trade Cycle (Oxford, 1961); preface of
1955 reprinted.

considered to help explain the Depression, but not its "full severity."[6] In general, he avoided flat concurrence with stagnationism and appealed to accelerator effects for the transition from high prosperity to Depression. He felt that the investment of the 1920's was highly dependent on a volume of consumer durables purchases "that could not be maintained indefinitely."[7] Though he granted that some overinvestment in auto factories, housing, and other fields had obtained, Gordon saw more essential deflationary influences in the diminishing growth rates in those industries. He added that financial factors had aggravated the Contraction (international imbalance, stock market instability, and vulnerability of the American banking system to panic). He denied that any rigorous abstract model, such as stagnationist or accelerator theory provided, was sufficiently complex to explain the Breakdown.[8] And yet Gordon's interpretation at this time represented the closest thing to a reconstruction of Clark's ideas which

---

[6]Robert A. Gordon, "Cyclical Experience in the Interwar Period," in Conference on Business Cycles (New York, N.B.E.R., 1951), 211.

[7]Ibid., 212.

[8]Ibid., 214-215.

had appeared since <u>Strategic Factors</u>. Without argumenta-
tion or flourish, Gordon had allowed the accelerator
approach to take its place as a fulcrum balancing the
conceptions of Schumpeter and Hansen. The problem of
slowing growth rates in a consumer-oriented market
replaced strict characterization of the technological
determinants of investment.

However, Gordon's attitudes had clearly changed
by the time of the 1961 edition of his general text
<u>Business Fluctuations</u>. Now (considering accelerator
effects as subordinate matters) he gave primary weight
to the financial factors, domestic and international,
in explaining the Collapse.[9] Discussing the incomplete
recovery of the thirties separately, Gordon pointed to
several factors--the aftermath of financial crisis, prior
overinvestment, and relative restriction of new outlets
for investment. On this last, Gordon sought compromise
between Schumpeter and Hansen: Hansen was right that
outlets were partly stagnant in the thirties, Schumpeter
was right that secular stagnation as a future condition
could not be argued from a short interlude such as the
thirties.[10] Further compromising, Gordon held that

---

[9]Gordon, <u>Business Fluctuations</u> (rev. ed., New
York, 1961), 446-447.

[10]<u>Ibid</u>., 448-449.

technological bases of stagnation had been less important
than declining population growth and consequent weakness
in the building industry. He cited some of Hansen's own
postwar work, and indicated that Hansen and himself were
gravitating toward the notion that the thirties had been
an episode theoretically comparable with the 1870's and
1890's.[11] Only the decline of population growth was a
really new circumstance. This in turn evidently would
explain, along with special postwar financial factors,
what Gordon had described at the outset: the unprecedented statistical extremity of the Depression.[12]

In short, Gordon now viewed the thirties from
such a distance that their stagnation did not seem portentous or really worthy of debate. He concluded,
brusquely, that one could never know whether government
spending had been the sine qua non of recent prosperity.[13]
His earlier accelerator-oriented interpretation had mediated between Schumpeter and Hansen in such a way as to
suggest, if not to argue, a dangerous new cyclicality
(due particularly to the dominance of consumer durables).
He had closely apprehended the fears of the writers of
the thirties, and worked as they worked to develop the

---

[11]Ibid., 448.

[12]Ibid., 428.

[13]Ibid., 450.

most dynamic possibilities of economic theory. Now,
impressed by postwar prosperity, stability, technology,
and population growth, he was, as were many economists,
reluctant to describe the interwar setbacks as deeply
expressive of the whole, matured economy of the time.

Around 1950, then, the work of Gordon and Hicks
exemplified a rather evanescent tendency toward the
development of accelerator theory as the touchstone of
a new conception of economics.[14] It should be emphasized again that contemporary economic stabilization set
the stage for the decline of the accelerator orientation.
Probably the most influential empirical study of the
determinants of investment, written in the postwar
period, is that of Meyer and Glauber--which treats and
generalizes upon material entirely from the 1950's.
The authors cogently documented the need for pluralism
of approach in explaining the volume of investment.
They concluded that accelerator-oriented information
(the rate of change of sales) was important, as well as

---

[14]For another, and important, example of revived
interest in acceleration, see the article R. Eckaus, "The
Acceleration Principle Reconsidered," Quarterly Journal
of Economics, v. 67, May 1953, 209-230. Eckaus urged
that the accelerator construction was wholly compatible
with the then ascendant concern with levels of the
capital stock. In general, he held that the accelerator
had been overly criticized.

measurements of business liquidity, and the level of
interest rates. But most vital were the levels of
utilization of industrial capacity, and indexes of
general expectations, as provided by security prices.[15]
They urged, finally, that theoretical openness to various interpretations for different occasions was essential.[16] Their study, so illuminating as to the 1950's,
was representative of the painstaking focus that was
informing the whole discipline of postwar economics.
That their models were dealing with an economy
stabilized by government spending, ought to have made
them virtually uninteresting for students of the interwar years. Unfortunately there was no such exclusive
study body. Gordon, Hansen, and the other formers of
opinion on the past, were all primarily absorbed in the
practice of current cycle analysis.

Hansen, in the early sixties, was playing an
influential role in characterizing the economy as in
need of heightened governmental stimulus. The only
addition to Hansen's reprinted text on business cycles,
of 1964, dealt with this problem and the postwar period

---

[15]John R. Meyer and R. R. Glauber, _Investment
Decisions, Economic Forecasting, and Public Policy_
(Boston, 1964), 247-249.

[16]_Ibid._, 251.

in general. For the rest, Hansen entirely reprinted his
text of 1951 and retained its title, Business Cycles and
National Income. Thus Hansen's contribution to interpretation of the past was preserved with a flavor of 1950.
He had come by that time to an increased concern with
accelerator principle, akin both to portions of his work
of 1938 and to Gordon's work of 1950. Of course, Hansen
had since 1938 allowed acceleration important away in the
development of great new industries, and hence influenced
Gordon's method. In some respects Hansen by 1951 went as
far as Gordon toward an accelerator interpretation of the
interwar years. He described in detail the automobile
cycle of the twenties, wholly in the context of
accelerator effects (including how the slackening growth
of auto purchases reacted upon investment in the auto
industry and in turn upon its subsidiaries). This was
one of the few real amplifications ever made upon Clark's
discussion of autos as of 1934.[17] Speaking later in
terms of cycle theory as a whole, Hansen submitted that
acceleration made cycles simply inevitable (barring

---

[17]Hansen, Business Cycles and National Income
(New York, 1964), 187-190. Another important reasser-
tion of the Clarkian idea of intensified acceleration
connected with consumer durables industries, may be
found in M. J. Farrell, "The New Theories of the
Consumption Function" (1959), reprinted in Readings in
Business Cycles, 1965.

government intervention)--since induced investment slows
as soon as the growth of overall output slows. The latter
circumstance seemed inevitable in the normal cycle, com-
mencing with a burst of activity.[18]

Still and all, Hansen never relinquished the
concept of autonomous investment as chiefly governing
business movements. He explained matters, with a kind
of irony, thus: when induced investment weakens late in
the boom, prosperity is rendered all the more dependent
on the continuance of autonomous investment. Hence,
when saturation of new outlets for autonomous investment
approaches--as it must--nothing remains to prevent contraction.[19] The Keynesian sense of absolute limitation
upon investment outlets stayed with Hansen, and continued
to master, though less easily, his attraction to accelerator theory. This was most palpable in Hansen's treatment of the interwar building cycle. He followed
Wilson's lead with a will: he argued that an unprecedented saturation of construction outlets obtained in
the late twenties. The consequent collapse in construction (intensified by population trends) he went on to
describe as the very soul of the severity of the
Depression.[20] Just as Gordon said in 1961, Hansen had

---

[18]Hansen, _Business Cycles and National Income_, 194.

[19]_Ibid._

[20]_Ibid._, 46-50.

largely decided that the stagnation of the thirties was
similar to that of the 1870's and 1890's. The coincident
and extreme building cycle (plus related demographic
problems) explained the bulk of the extra intensity of
the Depression relative to those others.[21]

The works of Hansen and Gordon around 1950
remain perhaps the last important interpretative
efforts in a broad deterministic vein. And Hansen's
appeal to unusual overinvestment in building, later taken
up by Gordon, already represented the trend toward dis-
aggregation or loosening of theoretical structures.
Long and Isard, it will be remembered, considered overspeculation to be a normal aspect of the building cycle.
Gordon, in fact, in 1950 had seen the housing boom of
the twenties as largely predictable, due both to the
opening of the suburbs and to general consumer prosperity.[22] As analysis slipped back into the parlance of
Mitchell in 1933, Keynes in 1936, Wilson in 1942,
lamenting aberrant overspeculation—it raised the question of why this had occurred, while making substantive
reply difficult. If the auto and suburbs had caused
speculative construction, then the latter was rather

---

[21]Ibid., 41.

[22]Gordon, "Cyclical Experience in the Interwar
Period," 212.

well founded. If it had caused itself, then it was an
unlikely fragment, unconducive to unifying interpretation. And it smacked of overcritical hindsight. One is
taken back to the somewhat awkward plight of Mitchell,
who admired the self-replicating processes of prosperity
in 1929, and bewailed overspeculation, on second thought,
in 1933.

Pluralistic economists of the postwar period
did develop sophisticated ways of loosely unifying such
observations. The work of James Duesenberry of 1958
provides an interesting example. Duesenberry designed
a cyclical model which accommodated several sorts of
factors, and was adaptable to different emphases for
different periods--an explicit antidote to the rigor of
Hick's accelerator model.[23] Duesenberry's model was
capable of picturing rather stable growth. While he
took exception with Hicks, and others, for overly dynamic
and cyclical conceptions, he considered Hansen's work to
be too grounded in autonomous investment, and too
devoted to the problem of fallings-off into depression.[24]
Duesenberry's method was not oriented to severe

[23]Duesenberry, Business Cycles and Economic
Growth (New York, 1958), 35-36.

[24]Ibid., 36-37, 48.

depressions; he treated them largely as the result of
extraordinary conditions, yielding "shocks" to the
economic system. In the 1920's the shocks had been
delivered severally, by the speculative cycles in housing and in securities, the rise and fall of large
foreign lending, agrarian depression, and the decrease
in population growth. The extremity of housing speculation he laid to initial postwar shortage, and to easy
mortgage conditions. He considered that the unusual
clustering of dangers was probably due to World War I;
at least the problems of foreign lending, agricultural
distress, and the housing boom were related to the War.[25]

This characterization was surely no large
advance over Mitchell's view as of 1933. But
Duesenberry sought also to suggest, briefly, the under-
lying conditions which proved so susceptible to these
shocks. Here Duesenberry gingerly applied the teachings
of Hansen. He described the autonomous impulses to
investment as weak in the 1920's relative to the
nineteenth century. Investment in public utility and
transport industries was now smaller as a proportion of
national product; and the great frontier developments
were finished. The automobile and related industries,

[25]Ibid., 288-294.

of course, had played a role analogous to railroads. But investment in these new fields had not so autonomous a thrust: for "it was not necessary to build so far ahead of demand."[26]

With this last statement, which Duesenberry did not develop, he had opened the way for a powerful accelerator interpretation of the entire cycle. As we have stressed, that investment was more closely correlated to current demand might have made for a wholly new dynamism in the economy of the twenties. Emphasis on this aspect of Duesenberry's argument might render it highly compact. But Duesenberry preferred loose articulation; in the end he was not sure whether the Great Depression would have occurred without the antecedent speculative episodes.[27] In any case, he took the step which Hansen had taken in 1938, viewing the prosperity of the twenties as largely unsound and artificial. Yet neither he nor Hansen had ever supposed that the development of the automobile was unsound or speculative. That it entailed a volatile, non-autonomous form of investment, rendered it the reverse of speculative: it would not go forward if income ceased expanding. Perhaps speculation in housing was greater than normal, having

---

[26]Ibid., 288.

[27]Ibid., 293-294.

become attuned to the rise of automobiles. Viewing
matters thus, one arrives at a not overly binding
synthesis: that the auto opened so promising a long-
term field for housing as to precipitate over-building,
even as auto investment became increasingly short-term.
Then a temporary decline in housing could have brought
on a sharp contraction in auto and other activity. Thus
a strong sense of interrelation may be maintained, as
well as a sense of the characteristic reflexes of
different segments of the economy.

Recent analysis often thus suggested integrative
possibilities, even while it studiously held off from
them. The reason for this was almost explicit in
Duesenberry's case. He was building a model that was
tailored for current use and not for the 1920's, for
mild cycles and not for explosive ones. Hence, in
adjusting for the 1920's, he was led to construe some of
the explosive elements as "speculative" and extrinsic--
temporary offsets to a weakened autonomous investment.
Yet investment in auto and electric facilities had
surged in the early twenties, and only grown hesitant
later in the decade. Clark's interpretation of 1934 was
still closest to the pulse of the twenties boom. He
had pictured the surge in autos and housing as mutually
reinforcing, and leading the economy, via acceleration,
to speculative heights. (Clark, in fact, had seen ways

of incorporating the stock market mania into a rational
pattern. While treating matters of money supply and
general optimism, which had always been adduced in discussions of the stock boom qua exceptional escapade--he
had added more. He asserted that the same accelerated
growth which had kept short-cyclical recessions neglig-
ible in the twenties, had thus bred the joyous idea of
the "New Era" and attendant speculation.)[28]

In retrospect it is clear that the optimists of
the New Era were enthralled by a perfectly accurate
vision. They envisioned our own era by simple extrapola-
tion from quite tangible developments in their time.
They saw that the market for autos and for suburban housing was almost infinitely extensible, along with the
market for hosts of other new consumer goods. At the
same time, the means of production had entered a phase of
continual revolution, rather as Schumpeter and Terborgh
continued to insist despite the Collapse. This surety of
markets and means were what enabled investment to behave
in the early twenties with an even more autonomous energy
than in the railroad age. The dependence of investment,
on a market that surely could not continue to expand at
its initial rate, revealed itself later. In some

---

[28]Clark, Strategic Factors, 100.

sectors (housing, securities) long-range prospects had seemed so good as to prompt speculation out of accord with immediate prospects. These were simply premature speculations upon our own age, not evidences of social insanity. Detached men like Mitchell felt that prosperity might go on, as long as purchasing power continued to expand. The worst fears of the day were expressed by Clark's formulation, that a reduced rate of growth, after large expansion of durable capital, might mean contraction. This formulation itself was optimistic in that it supposed continued growth of consumption. The intractably dynamic dangers that it implied sprang from purely "technical" considerations. If ever a man spied out, with sheerest delicacy and without animus, the fatal paradox of his era--it was Clark.

*   *   *

It is only fitting that the fatal technicality, the inherent instability of the modern consumer durable goods economy, has been brought under control by the imposition of another quite as unfeeling technicality: wasteful government expenditure. One is of course tempted to suppose that the humane and critical tradition of Dewey, Veblen, and Tugwell will yet have its day.

Still, it does little good to insist that these men were
truly representative of the deepest drift of their contemporary American society. They were men who expressed
the hard utilitarian concerns of America along with a
sense of ideal standards entirely their own. Most
Americans undoubtedly sympathized with those standards
as distant objectives—but surely not as immediate ones.
The real springs of American pragmatism and instrumental-
ism were the ubiquitous material opportunities of her
environment. Similarly, the bases of political Progressiv-
ism, beneath the high-flown rhetoric of its leaders, lay
in a newly dominant urban middle class bent on more
strictly administering in its interests. Modern scholar-
ship has made these disappointing lessons ever clearer.
By the same token, it has generally tended to overturn
the inherited Progressive idea that the 1920's manifested
a peculiarly malignant and selfish spirit. We have gone
under the assumption in this paper that the 1920's
embodied a perfectly natural evolutionary step forward.
The growing sympathy of men like Tugwell and Mitchell
with the current regime of big business ought not to be
seen as a betrayal of their tradition. Business was
probably doing more for social justice than Progressive
politics had done.

When the Depression came, Mitchell and Tugwell
must have felt betrayed by business; and they felt a
revived Progressive anti-plutocratic bias. New Dealers
like Tugwell turned to that old politics as if they
contained the true pragmatic answers to economic problems. With hindsight, one can see that Progressive
rhetoric was more than ever irrelevant to political
reality when Roosevelt came to power. For business
itself had been forced into politics, and was inevitably
dominant in the proto-corporate state of N.R.A. More
importantly, by the 1920's the common materialistic
philosophy of the society had been fully revealed, as
business, labor and middle classes shared prosperity
avidly and with a new mutuality. Though for a twinkling
in the late twenties this seemed unclear--by 1933 control
of the business cycle had emerged as the focal problem
of American pragmatism. Everyone had risen together,
and fallen together. Though social friction and
recrimination naturally blossomed in the unfortunate
thirties, it blossomed everywhere. Economists could
make a case against high wages as readily as against
underconsumption. Most could agree that the international financial crisis had been partly at fault; yet
autarchy was more readily embraced than liberal free
trade, as things turned out.

The logic of the situation in the wake of the twenties, then, did not call for interpretations and remedies based on institutionalism, so largely a class-oriented Progressive methodology. Yet of course, from a strictly moral viewpoint, capitalism had done enough damage and ought to have been entirely reconstructed. Hence, reformist institutionalism dominated intellectual circles as never before. The poignancy of this is great. Reconstruction did not occur; in fact, society had been so shaken that it failed even to mobilize a real bout of government spending. All the more intellectual credit must go to Clark, who returned to business cycle interpretation with renewed energy, and yet maintained the highest continuity in his work. He, as much as Tugwell, had been a scion of liberal institutionalism, and a bold proponent of social control. He continued to be these. But from 1917 he had labored to extrude the institutionalist perception (of the imperfection of capitalism) to the point where it might bear on the most global and incorrigible motions of capitalism. And when the collapse into Depression seemed almost to pull apart the ordinarily steadfast Mitchell (he stressed the exceptional financial causes of the Depression, yet mused that utter underconsumption might be the point after all)--Clark gave the National Bureau his

<u>Strategic Factors</u>, a concentrated advance in the interpretation of dynamic cycles. It was of course precisely suited to its date of publication: for in 1934 the full course of the cycle had been run. Its extremes cried out for explanation at any cost, including the renovation of the whole field of economics.

We have suggested that the accelerator approach of Clark was dynamic to the point of undermining much of the traditionally absolutistic perceptions of economics, as practiced a generation ago and even now. We have added that the socioeconomic developments of the 1920's and 1930's are seen most faithfully as a paradigm of cyclical, and not continuous or structural, problems. However justly motivated the absolutistic critique of capitalism in the early 1930's, it was unconvincing to the extent that it did not fairly encompass the strengths of the 1920's. Clark's method did encompass these strengths, and how they were necessarily transformed into weaknesses, without laboring to show them as delusive or tainted from the start. Nor did he rely on the homily (as Keynes did) that after too great a feast there will be famine. Clark went to the heart of the particular pragmatic question of the day: what made prosperity newly self-reversing in the twenties? How had economic data which used to have absolute connotations become fundamentally relative to their position in the course of the business cycle?

An increasingly dynamic capitalism bred an increasingly relativistic culture. The pragmatism of William James, despite its moral sensitivity, was rich in subjectivism and relativism. These elements seemed for a time to be at odds with the great empiricism and materialism of the pragmatic outlook. In the American 1920's the full connections were revealed. For finally the whole pursuit of material needs, the patterns of investment and consumption, could be seen to have no absolute foundations. Keynes, from an early date, urged that wasteful expenditure was a valid way of insuring advances in production and the satisfaction of needs. He was, however, not closely enough attuned to American experience to fathom the extent to which the structure of social needs had become intangible and relative to economic trends. Only Clark truly touched upon the bizarre and utter fusion that had come about between pragmatic materialism and pragmatic relativism in the American social organism.

The work of Keynesians, particularly Hansen, drove home the point in a powerful but negative way. Investment was no longer sufficiently autonomous to warrant prosperity. This idea, from its prefigurement in Roosevelt's Commonwealth Club speech, encouraged rather sweeping views of a disastrous transition to maturity in the American economy. These views, developed especially by Keynesians, led straightforwardly enough to the proposition that a moribund investment must be replaced by government spending. What Keynes and Hansen did not really divine was the amazing expansion that would be induced in investment, given a consistent policy of government stimulatory expenditure. Foster and Catchings, in their recommendations of the 1920's, had embodied an even truer avant-guarde: they saw the economy as newly blessed by the purchase of inessential goods, and urged that spending be artificially supported. They were outside traditional economic analysis, and emphasized consumption rather than investment. This in itself represented an American tendency. Investment-oriented schools would never fully explain the American twenties until they grasped the ways in which consumption had intensified the investment cycle. Clark's method accomplished the bridge, of course, and not the gloomier European schools of underconsumption. Post-Keynesian accelerator-multiplier models made economic stimulation and control a quasi-scientific pursuit. Thus, not merely a negative reaction away from the 1930's was developed, but a positive reconstruction of the desired aspects of the 1920's.

This was a profound vindication of the central
insight of Schumpeter, perhaps more than of his perpetu-
ally ascendant rivals Keynes and Hansen. Schumpeter,
the non-revolutionary counterpart of Marx in this
century, had constructed a theory of economic history
even more suited to American than to European conditions.
His coming to America, and prominence here, was a
splendid symbol of the passage of world economic leadership in the same direction, clear enough by World War I.
The emphasis of Schumpeter, and other Continental
economists such as Spiethoff, had embodied perhaps the
most important refutation of Marx ever systematically
evolved. This was that capitalism, rather than a
fetter upon the development of means of production, was
enslaved to this latter process; and that its weaknesses,
especially cyclical failure, were temporary sacrifices to
developmental ends. Marx had written when the propulsive
force of technology was less fully and evenly felt than
it came to be by the turn of the century and after.
Spiethoff already emphasized, in a proto-Keynesian
fashion, the depressions that could accompany a temporary
slackening in the pace of technological change.
Schumpeter saw instead a gathering forward energy in
technology, and was the incontestable seer of the period
1900 to 1929 (viewed as a whole, and with stress upon

America). Mitchell was inevitably drawn to Schumpeterian
formulations of the period leading up to 1929 (advance of
technology, high competition between new and old
industries, etc.).

The 1930's promised Spiethoff his first American
fanfare; and Hansen and Schumpeter argued closely from
the two wings of the technological interpretation. As
we have argued, neither was wholly correct, and mediation
was required from Clark's contribution. Both Schumpeter
and Hansen showed signs of accepting this, most explicitly
Hansen, when he made his accelerator interpretation of the
grisly setback of 1937-38. But for the larger transition
of 1929, Schumpeter's grand, procrustean, and even
tortured characterization, held an essential truth.
Somehow, the explosive progress of technology was itself
to blame, rather than its alleged sudden failure to
create investment. Technology had developed new outlets,
especially in consumer durables, which could guarantee a
virtually infinite growth of demand. The mobilization
of savings and credit to satisfy those demands reached
an intensity in the initial stages which promised severe
correction as rates of expansion slowed. And with
investment following demand as never before, correction
became interminable contraction. A fundamentally new
stage in economic history had been reached, which did
not correspond to Schumpeter's idea of cyclical

investment determination. Competition, the immemorial
mechanism of economic adjustment, had been replaced by
acceleration. But though investment outlets were now
relative and not absolute, they were unquestionably
present. As to technological history, the current regime
of artificial stabilization has served to bear out
Schumpeter's deepest optimism.

Keynes and Hansen, of course, made the vital
pragmatic step, arguing from the lack of (autonomous)
investment to the need for government spending. Hansen,
in turn, quickly surpassed Keynes in the historical interpretation of the demise of autonomous investment. Hansen
elaborated with more American sensibility, the precarious
dependence of basic investment upon innovation. Furthermore, Hansen first enduringly bound accelerator method to
the investment-based interpretation of cycles. On both
grounds, he may be seen to have moved more readily to a
dynamic conception of things than his mentor Keynes.
Nor did he deny that American technology remained
potently progressive: ultimately he only doubted that
fortuitously grand advances like the auto would be
repeated soon enough. He could be said to have developed
a most dynamic view of cycle history, in that he considered constant and turbulent change in levels of
activity to be dictated by the very nature of

technological (and demographic) history. But his conception probably explained the checkered course of
nineteenth century economics better than the monumental
turnabout of the 1920's. And he resisted the the development of dynamic economics to the point of full relativism, which Clark had broached.

The dynamic relativism of Clark gave perhaps a
truer clue than Keynesianism to the nature of the reforms
that were required, and finally made, for the preserva-
tion of capitalism. Not merely the guaranteed levels of
government spending were important, but the high rates of
taxation they entailed: these set new limits to the
upward motions of income due to accelerator-multiplier
effects.[29] Interestingly, on the question of reform,
Clark had not been drawn to government spending as a
large solution. As we have seen, Clark in 1934 hewed to
the institutionalist vision, recommending direct government control of durables output. He continued wary of
Keynesian government works as disruptive to private
investment; in 1945 he added that such projects would
merely increase an already dangerous preponderance of
durable goods. Hence he suggested withholding of public

---

[39]Cf. Hansen's discussion of the "built-in
stabilizers" of government postwar taxation and spending, in Hansen, Business Cycles, 1964.

works till after the inevitable postwar boom in durables faltered.[30] He remained faithful to his original characterization of the Collapse, then, but could not entirely conceive the government spending-and-taxation remedy which it implied.

Clark's advice of 1934, of course, represented an adaptation of institutionalist reformism to the specific problems of the business cycle. Even in this it was clear that he had worked to recast the structural critique of institutionalism into a cyclical mode. He could hardly have foreseen the dimensions of the relativism that would engulf the American socioeconomic scene-- whereby the whole tradition of rational social reform was inundated and submerged in an artificially generated stream of purchasing power. Still buoyed by this, American society appears at length to have returned to scrutiny of her institutions in terms of absolute moral standards. It will likely be found that such standards can much better be served during prosperity than during the sort of cataclysm which surrounded the efforts of New Deal radicals. The essentially static critical method of Progressive and pragmatic institutionalism will

---

[30]Clark, "Financing High-Level Employment" in Financing American Prosperity, Twentieth Century Fund (New York, 1945), 87-89.

revive on congenial grounds, in the stabilized contemporary economy. But the vast and jagged interlude from 1920 to 1940, in which America struggled on the threshold of maturity, simply defied the modes of critical analysis which had grown up in the first flush of revulsion from mechanistic classical economics. The best testament to the resourcefulness of institutionalist tradition was that Clark had been able, working unequivocally from within it, to transform it. Further, of course, the interwar transformation--in matters of fact and of theory--was a distinctly American development, and quite impossible outside the context of American material progress and pragmatic culture.

BIBLIOGRAPHY

For this thesis, the distinction between primary and secondary sources is particularly difficult. Since we have treated the major interpretative works of economic history, even the current ones, as primary sources themselves open to interpretation--the category of "secondary sources" is largely depleted. But as a rule the sources treated here have substantial "secondary" value, and increasingly as their dates of publication approach the postwar period. So, for example, Alvin Hansen's volume, Business Cycles and National Income (New York, 1964), (most written in 1951), while interestingly representing the thought of the early 1950's, is perhaps the most authoritative general secondary source for the material of this thesis. It not only gives a fine introduction to the history of business cycles in America, but explores the developing field of cycle theory from its origins around 1900. Since cycle theory has been the major embodiment of "dynamic" analysis, the point at which economic history and theory most centrally unite, both of the latter must be approached via cycle theory. Hence, the areas of focus of Hansen's book make it an ideal introduction to the subject of

this thesis. Further, it has a large and excellent
bibliography covering virtually every important contribution to macroeconomic analysis in this century. Other
fine works on the history and theory of cycles are
James S. Duesenberry, Business Cycles and Economic Growth
(New York, 1958); and R. C. O. Matthews, The Business
Cycle (Chicago, 1959). The former has a large mathematical content, but can be profitably used by the layman;
the latter is attuned to British experience, but has
valuable comparative aspects, and remarkable conciseness.
Neither book has a bibliography. (Nor do these works
have the orientation to the history of economic analysis,
which makes Hansen's book so rich.) For a broad sampling
of currents in postwar cycle analysis, there is nothing
more helpful than Readings in Business Cycles, American
Economic Association (Homewood, Ill., 1965). Finally,
there is Robert A. Gordon, Business Fluctuations (New
York, 1961)--useful on business cycles, and containing
rounded essays on American economic history, comparable
in value to those in Hansen's volume.

Outside the integrating focus of business cycle
theory, approaches to the subject of this thesis must,
of course, be made through the more conventional categories of history (including intellectual history and
economic history). Brief, general, and balanced

approaches to the 1920's are provided by John D. Hicks,
Republican Ascendancy, 1921-1933 (New York, 1960); and
William E. Leuchtenburg, The Perils of Prosperity, 1914-
1933 (Chicago, 1958). For the 1930's, no better concise
account exists than William E. Leuchtenburg, Franklin D.
Roosevelt and the New Deal, 1932-1940 (New York, 1963).
All three books have limited, but useful bibliographies
(including works on the interpretation of the Depression).
Richer intellectual background sketches, which were of
considerable use in the preparation of this thesis,
appear in the large work, Arthur M. Schlesinger, Jr.,
The Age of Roosevelt, 3 vols. (Boston, 1957, ff.)
Schlesinger has no bibliography, but good thick foot-
noting. Even in reading the above general works, there
is need for the brilliant analysis of thought in the
1920's--and the correctives to later bias against the
1920's--supplied by Henry F. May, "Shifting Perspectives
on the 1920's," Mississippi Valley Historical Review,
v. 43, December 1956, 405-427. May's effort is largely
to underscore the earnest, progressive aspects of the
optimism which pervaded the 1920's, and to expose the
charicatures which grow up after 1930.

As to the histories devoted to economic thought,
a few are sufficient, though no one alone can be. Broad
and detailed coverage up until 1933 is given by Joseph

Dorfman, <u>The Economic Mind in American Civilization</u>, v. 5
(New York, 1959). He treats all sorts of economists, but
not always equally cogently. The major strengths and
weaknesses of his work are related. His organization is
weak and confusing: but this looseness permits a very
fair and unstrained treatment of many figures. His work
on J. M. Clark is lengthy and good, if not very systematic.
His coverage of early interpretations of the Depression
is quite full (certainly fuller than that of this thesis)--
but, again, not well drawn together. Dorfman's footnotes
are not easy to use (for various reasons). Dorfman has
plenty of information on institutionalist economics, but
for a focused account it is necessary to consult Allan
G. Gruchy, <u>Modern Economic Thought: The American Contri-</u>
<u>bution</u> (New York, 1947). This deals separately with
Wesley Mitchell, Rexford Tugwell, J. M. Clark, John R.
Commons, and Gardiner Means. Gruchy makes a sometimes
strained effort to bind these men to the tradition of
Veblen; and the writing is long-winded. But the various
ideas which might be considered to embody "institutionalism" are exhaustively set forth, and their origins as
well. Gruchy does not deal much with his subjects'
interpretations of the Depression <u>per se</u>. But the basic
attitudes of the five men emerge clearly: and the
bibliography of their works is complete (up to 1947),

and hence indispensable.

But a swifter, and surer introduction to the elusive tradition of institutionalism may be found in the set of reprinted lectures in Institutional Economics (Berkeley, 1963). This includes a fine and dexterous essay by Joseph Dorfman on the early origins of institutionalism; a solid discussion of Wesley Mitchell by his colleague Simon Kuznets; a brilliantly ranging essay by Robert A. Gordon, called "Institutional Elements in Contemporary Economics"; and other material of some use. The essay by Neil W. Chamberlain on John R. Commons is very full. By demonstrating the highly sociological thrust of Commons' work, the essay serves as an explanation as to why Commons might be omitted in a study of economic interpretation (as he has been omitted in this study), without underestimating his contribution to social thought.

On Keynes, and the overall developments in economics to which he contributed, the best commentary is Lawrence Klein, The Keynesian Revolution (New York, 1966). It is important to use the recent edition, for the original work (of 1949) is preserved but expanded upon there. Klein in the second edition felt a diminished loyalty to Keynes' work per se, and stressed the limitations of The General Theory for dynamic (business cycle)

analysis. Klein is useful for the background of the
"revolution" as well as for its complex sequel. Some
of the book is technical, and difficult, and some of it
badly written. There is no bibliography, though many
writings are treated in the text. Unfortunately, discussion of the causes of the Depression is limited.
Whatever its shortcomings, Klein's book is a vitally
authoritative study in economic thought. A broad
supplement to it is provided by Seymour Harris, ed.,
The New Economics: Keynes' Influence on Theory and
Public Policy (New York, 1965). This work has not the
consistent and unified approach of Klein, but presents
valuable essays on various topics by leading economists.
For explication of The General Theory itself, the
standard reference is Alvin Hansen, A Guide to Keynes
(New York, 1953). This also contains some useful discussion of related works in economics, before and after
Keynes.

There are more general histories of modern
economic analysis, though none is so important for
macroeconomics as Klein. A fine study of economics from
the middle ages through Keynes is Eric Roll, A History
of Economic Thought (Englewood Cliffs, 1956). This
contains much difficult microeconomic material, including
the school of "imperfect competition" which flourished
after 1930. But there is a good brief summary of the

debate over stagnation, and other questions of interest
for broad economic interpretation. Probably the fullest
background work is Joseph Schumpeter, History of Economic
Analysis (New York, 1954). Tragically, Schumpeter's
death truncated the work, leaving its treatment of major
developments after 1914 in a sketchy, though suggestive,
form. On Schumpeter himself, a full range of evaluative
positions is presented in the essays of Seymour Harris, ed.
Schumpeter: Social Scientist (Cambridge, Mass., 1951).
But this is well supplemented by Robert A. Gordon, in
the course of his essay "Institutional Elements in
Contemporary Economics," in Institutional Economics
(Berkeley, 1963). Finally, there is a classic study of
business cycle theory up to 1936, Gottfied Haberler,
Prosperity and Depression (New York, 1937, 1958). This
work, together with the writings on Schumpeter, provides
a helpful offset to the essentially Keynes-centered
works, such as Klein, which must remain the key secondary sources.

On the concrete economic history of America in
this century, the sources are surprisingly thin and
scattered. The reader is cautioned that without reference to Hansen, Business Cycles and National Income, and
the other basic texts on cycle history cited above, one's
preparation must be incomplete. An indispensable aid is

Seymour Harris, ed., <u>American Economic History</u> (New York, 1961). But this compilation contains essays on such a range of material, as to preclude intensive treatment of the period 1920 to 1940. Entirely inadequate are the standard historical surveys: Henry F. Williamson, <u>Growth of the American Economy</u> (Englewood Cliffs, 1951), and Edward C. Kirkland, <u>A History of American Economic Life</u> (New York, 1951). For historians, probably the most influential secondary source on the origins of the Depression has been George Soule, <u>Prosperity Decade: From War to Depression: 1917-1929</u> (New York, 1947). This book does represent a useful introduction to the economic questions of the period. But the author is too concerned with a reevaluation of the old Progressive or institutionalist price-critique (which he ultimately largely relinquishes). His knowledge of other approaches is good, but his rendition of them cannot be considered authoritative as of 1947, or later. Hence the book was not treated in this thesis. Had it been treated, it would have partly stood for the unquestionable lag which has opened up between interpretation in the economics profession, and interpretation in other academic disciplines. Notably in history, the tendency to cling to Progressive notions has been stubborn: it makes a decided contribution to the Schlesinger account

of the Age of Roosevelt, and to later works, even though
historians have not been dogmatic about it. The flexibility of Keynesian economics, of course, has allowed a
certain immunity for neo-Progressive orientations (particularly underconsumptionism); and such views have been
partly reinforced by the liberal economist John K.
Galbraith's, The Great Crash, 1929 (Boston, 1954). But
Soule's book was published earlier, and remains the most
direct influence. Its competence in treating the substantive, or structural aspects of the 1920's has over-
ridden its limitations on the dynamic, interpretative
problems. In any event, it contains an excellent and
large bibliographical essay. And it is surely better
grounded interpretatively than its sequel (in the series
The Economic History of the United States)--Broadus
Mitchell, Depression Decade (New York, 1947).

To round out the bibliography on economic history
in 1920-1940, we must return to works discussed in this
thesis as "primary sources." To name a few of the best
chronologically: Frederick C. Mills, Economic Tendencies
in the United States (New York, 1932); J. M. Clark,
Strategic Factors in Business Cycles (New York, 1934);
Joseph Schumpeter, Business Cycles, v. 2 (New York, 1939);
Thomas Wilson, Fluctuations in Income and Employment
(London, 1942); Walter Isard, "Transport Development and
Building Cycles," Quarterly Journal of Economics, v. 57,

November 1942; and (most important of all) Robert A. Gordon, "Cyclical Experience in the Interwar Period, in Conference on Business Cycles (New York, N.B.E.R., 1951). As to the strictly financial aspects of the period, consult, among others, Milton Friedman and A. J. Schwartz, A Monetary History of the United States, 1867-1960 (New York, 1963), and Harold Barger, The Management of Money (Chicago, 1964).

There are two books which have made important impressions on the general academic readership outside the economic profession. Both are brilliant, but view the world crisis of the thirties from a distinctly English or internationalist standpoint (reminiscent of the conception of Keynes' Treatise on Money of 1930). They are Karl Polanyi, The Great Transformation (New York, 1944), and W. Arthur Lewis, Economic Survey 1919-1939 (London, 1949). Lewis remains the finest authority on the international aspects of the Depression. Polanyi's book, like Schumpeter's Capitalism, Socialism, and Democracy (New York, 1942), remains an inspired synthesis in history and economics, all too neglected now, but to be read with caution.

Some recent works require mention. Robert T. Patterson, The Great Boom and Panic (Chicago, 1965), runs parallel to Galbriath's The Great Crash, analyzing

the financial excesses of the twenties and only briefly
treating the larger origins of the Depression. It is
not an improvement on Galbraith's book, but a step backward, due to diffuseness and interpretative hesitancy.
Murray Rothbard, America's Great Depression (Princeton,
1963), amounts to a pure anomaly: it argues, unskill-
fully, a financial interpretation based on the works of
certain Austrian economists now little read. On the
other hand, Ellis W. Hawley, The New Deal and the Problem
of Monopoly (Princeton, 1966), is a fine and intensive
study of structural problems in industry during the
1930's. Hawley does not claim to make a general interpretative contribution to the literature on the Depression. Used with this proviso, his work should become a
classic reference book for historians.

The writings listed below certainly do not
comprise an exhaustive Bibliography on the Depression.
But the most influential, and the most cogent, expres-
sions of the various viewpoints are adequately represented. The division between "Primary" and "Secondary"
materials has been set at 1946. As noted above, many--
perhaps most--of the works published earlier retain value
as secondary sources. But the works since the War do
fairly consistently serve better to introduce the problems of the Depression in perspective. In fact, the
arbitrary date of 1946 has worked surprisingly well in

separating the more polemical writings from the calmer
ones (if not the duller from the brilliant).

Primary Sources

Adams, Arthur B. The Trend of Business 1922-1932.
New York, 1932.

_____. Analyses of Business Cycles. New York, 1936.

American Economic Association. Readings in Business
Cycle Theory. Philadelphia, 1944.

Arndt, H. W. The Economic Lessons of the 1930's.
London, 1944.

Ayres, Clarence E. "The Impact of the Great Depression
on Economic Thinking," American Economic Review,
v. 36, May 1946, 112-125.

Ayres, Leonard P. The Economics of Recovery. New York,
1934.

Beard, Charles A., ed. America Faces the Future.
Boston, 1932.

Berle, Adolf A., Jr. and Gardiner C. Means. The Modern
Corporation and Private Property. New York,
1933.

Berle, Adolf A., Jr., et al. America's Recovery Program.
London, 1934.

Berle, Adolf A., Jr. "A High Road for Business,"
Scribner's Magazine, v. 93, June 1933, 325-332.

Black, John D. "The Agricultural Situation," Review of
Economic Statistics, v. 15, January 1933, 27-35.

Brown, Douglass V., et al. The Economics of the
Recovery Program. New York, 1934.

Burns, Arthur F. Production Trends in the United States
since 1870. New York, N.B.E.R., 1934.

Burns, Arthur R. The Decline of Competition. New York, 1936.

Burns, E. M. "Institutionalism and Orthodox Economics," American Economic Review, v. 21, March 1931, 80-87.

Chamberlin, Edward. The Theory of Monopolistic Competition. Cambridge, Mass., 1933.

Chase, Stuart. Prosperity--Fact or Myth? New York, 1929.

_____. The Nemesis of American Business and Other Essays. New York, 1931.

_____. A New Deal. New York, 1932.

_____. The Economy of Abundance. New York, 1934.

Clark, John Maurice. Studies in the Economics of Overhead Costs. Chicago, 1923.

_____. Social Control of Business. Chicago, 1926.

_____. The Costs of the War to the American People. New Haven, 1931.

_____. Strategic Factors in Business Cycles. New York, N.B.E.R., 1934.

_____. The Economics of Planning Public Works. Washington, 1935.

_____. Social Control of Business, expanded and revised. Chicago, 1939.

_____. "The Relation Between Statics and Dynamics," in Jacob E. Hollander, ed., Economic Essays in Honor of John Bates Clark. New York, 1927.

_____. "Capital Production and Consumer-Taking: A Reply," Journal of Political Economy, v. 39, December 1931, 814-816.

_____. "Capital Production and Consumer-Taking: A Further Word," Journal of Political Economy, v. 40, October 1932, 691-693.

_____. "Convulsion in the Price Structure," Yale Review, v. 22, March 1933, 496-510.

Clark, John Maurice, et al., in conference on "Institutional Economics," <u>American Economic Review</u>,
v. 22, March 1932, 105-116.

Commons, John R. <u>Institutional Economics: Its Place in
Political Economy</u>, 2 v. New York, 1934.

Crowther, Samuel, <u>et al</u>. <u>A Basis for Stability</u>. Boston,
1932.

Derksen, J. B. D. "Long Cycles in Residential Building:
An Explanation," <u>Econometrica</u>, v. 8, April 1940,
97-117.

Douglas, Paul H. <u>Controlling Depressions</u>. New York,
1935.

Ely, Richard T. <u>Hard Times: The Way in and the Way Out</u>.
New York, 1931.

Epstein, Ralph C. <u>Industrial Profits in the United
States</u>. New York, N.B.E.R., 1934.

Fellner, William. "The Technological Argument of the
Stagnation Thesis," <u>Quarterly Journal of
Economics</u>, v. 55, August 1941, 638-641.

Fisher, Irving. <u>The Stock Market Crash--and After</u>.
New York, 1930.

_____. <u>Booms and Depressions</u>. New York, 1932.

_____. "Our Unstable Dollar and the So-Called Busi-
ness Cycle," <u>Journal of the American Statistical
Association</u>, v. 20, June 1925, 179-202.

_____. "The Debt-Deflation Theory of Great
Depressions," <u>Econometrica</u>, v. 1, October 1933,
337-350.

Foster, William Trufant and Waddill Catchings.
<u>Business Without a Buyer</u>. Boston, 1927.

_____. <u>The Road to Plenty</u>. Boston, 1928.

_____. "Must We Reduce Our Standard of Living?"
<u>Forum</u>, v. 85, February 1931, 74-79.

_____. "In the Day of Adversity," <u>Atlantic Monthly</u>,
v. 148, July 1931, 101-106.

252

Foster, William Trufant. "When a Horse Balks," <u>North American Review</u>, v. 234, July 1932, 4-10.

Frankfurter, Felix. "Social Issues Before the Supreme Court," <u>Yale Review</u>, v. 22, March 1933, 476-496.

Frisch, Ragnar. "The Interrelation Between Capital Production and Consumer-Taking," <u>Journal of Political Economy</u>, v. 39, October 1931, 646-654.

_____. "Capital Production and Consumer-Taking: A Rejoinder," <u>Journal of Political Economy</u>, v. 40, April 1932, 253-255.

_____. "Capital Production and Consumer-Taking: A Final Word," <u>Journal of Political Economy</u>, v. 40, October, 1932, 694.

Gayer, Arthur D. <u>Monetary Policy and Economic Stabilization</u>. London, 1935.

Hamilton, Walton H. "The Control of Big Business," <u>Nation</u>, v. 134, May 25, 1932, 591-593.

Hansen, Alvin H. <u>Business-Cycle Theory: Its Development and Present Status</u>. Boston, 1927.

_____. <u>Economic Stabilization in an Unbalanced World</u>. New York, 1932.

_____. <u>Full Recovery or Stagnation?</u> New York, 1938.

_____. <u>Fiscal Policy and Business Cycles</u>. New York, 1941.

_____. "Mr. Keynes on Underemployment Equilibrium," <u>Journal of Political Economy</u>, v. 44, October 1936, 667-686.

_____. "Some Notes on Terborgh's <u>The Bogey of Economic Maturity</u>," <u>Review of Economic Statistics</u>, v. 28, February 1946, 13-17.

Harris, Seymour E., ed. <u>Postwar Economic Problems</u> New York, 1943.

Harrod, Roy F. <u>The Trade Cycle</u>. Oxford, 1936.

Hodson, H. V. <u>The Economics of a Changing World</u>. New York, 1933.

Hugh-Jones, E. M., and E. A. Radice. An American Experiment. London, 1936.

Isard, Walter. "Transport Development and Building Cycles," Quarterly Journal of Economics, v. 57, November 1942, 90-112.

Kahn, R. F. "The Relation of Home Investment to Unemployment," Economic Journal, v. 41, June 1931, 173-198.

Keynes, John Maynard. A Treatise on Money, 2 v. New York, 1930.

_____. Essays in Persuasion. London, 1931.

_____. The General Theory of Employment, Interest, and Money. New York, 1936.

Keynes, John Maynard, et al. The World's Economic Crisis and the Way of Escape. London, 1932.

Kuznets, Simon. National Income and Capital Formation, 1919-1935. New York, N.B.E.R., 1937.

_____. Economic Change: Selected Essays in Business Cycles, National Income, and Economic Growth. New York, 1953.

Leven, Maurice et al. America's Capacity to Consume. Washington, 1934, Brookings Institute.

Lippmann, Walter. Interpretations, 1931-1932. New York, 1932.

_____. "A Reckoning: Twelve Years of Republican Rule," Yale Review, v. 21, June 1932, 649-660.

Long, Clarence D., Jr. Building Cycles and the Theory of Investment. Princeton, 1940.

Macfie, Alec L. Theories of the Trade Cycle. London, 1934.

Mason, Edward S. "Price Inflexibility," Review of Economic Statistics, v. 20, May 1938, 53-64.

Means, Gardiner C. "The Large Corporation in American Life," American Economic Review, v. 21, March 1931, 10-37.

_____. "The Consumer and the New Deal," Annals of the American Academy of Politics and Social Science, v. 173, May 1934, 7-17.

_____. "Notes on Inflexible Prices," American Economic Review, v. 26, March 1936, 23-35.

Mills, Frederick C. Economic Tendencies in the United States. New York, N.B.E.R., 1932.

_____. Prices in Recession and Recovery. New York, N.B.E.R., 1936.

Mitchell, Wesley, C. Business Cycles. Berkeley, 1913.

_____. Business Cycles--The Problem and Its Setting. New York, N.B.E.R., 1927.

_____. "Review," in Report on Recent Economic Change, in the United States. New York, N.B.E.R., 1929, v. 2, 842-910.

_____. "Review of Findings," in Report on Recent Social Trends in the United States. New York, President's Research Committee on Social Trends, 1934, i-lxxv.

_____. "Business Cycles," World Today, October 1933, 28.

Naess, Ragnar D. "A Quantitative Study of Economic Balance," Harvard Business Review, v. 12, April 1934, 284-296.

New Republic, symposium on "The Depression," New Republic, v. 93, February 2, 1938, 377-393.

Newman, William H. The Building Industry and Business Cycles. Chicago, 1935.

Nourse, Edwin G., et al. America's Capacity to Produce. Washington, 1934, Brookings Institute.

Polanyi, Karl. The Great Transformation. New York, 1934.

John R. "Building Cycles in the United
ites, 1875-1932," American Statistical
   iociation, v. 28, June 1933, 174-183.

Robbins, Lionel. The Great Depression. London, 1934.

Roosevelt, Franklin D., Rosenman, Samuel, ed. The
Public Papers and Addresses of Franklin D.
Roosevelt, v. 1, New York, 1938.

Rorty, Col. Malcolm C. "How May Business Revival be
Forced?" Harvard Business Review (special
Supp.), v. 10, April 1932, 385-398.

_____. "The Equation of Economic Balance," Harvard
Business Review, v. 12, April, 1934, 274-283.

Salter, Sir Arthur. "The World Financial Crisis," Yale
Review, v. 21, December 1931, 217-232.

Samuelson, Paul. "Interactions Between the Multiplier
Analysis and the Principle of Acceleration,"
Review of Economic Statistics, v. 21, May 1939,
75-79.

Schumpeter, Joseph A. The Theory of Economic Development.
Cambridge, Mass., 1934.

_____. Business Cycles, A Theoretical, Historical,
and Statistical Analysis of the Capitalist
Process, 2 v. New York, 1939.

_____. "The Present World Depression: A Tentative
Diagnosis," American Economic Review, v. 21,
Supp., March 1931, 179-182.

_____. "The Analysis of Economic Change," Review of
Economic Statistics, v. 17, May 1935, 2-10.

_____. "The Decade of the 1920's," American Economic
Review, Proceedings, v. 36, May 1946, 1-10.

Slichter, Sumner H. Towards Stability. New York, 1934.

_____. "The Period 1919-1936 in the United States:
Its Significance for Business Cycle Theory,"
Review of Economic Statistics, v. 19, February
1937, 1-16.

_____. "The Downturn of 1937," Review of Economic Statistics, v. 20, August 1938, 97-110.

Smith, J. G., ed. Facing the Facts. New York, 1932.

Soule George. A Planned Society. New York, 1932.

_____. The Coming American Revolution. New York, 1934.

Tebbutt, Arthur R. "The Behavior of Consumption in Business Depression," Business Research Studies, No. 3, 1933, 1-21.

Terborgh, George. The Bogey of Economic Maturity. Chicago, 1945.

_____. "Dr. Hansen on The Bogey of Economic Maturity," Review of Economic Statistics, v. 28, April 1946, 170-171.

Tinbergen, Jan. "Statistical Evidence on the Acceleration Principle," Economica, v. 5, May 1938, 164-175.

Tugwell, Rexford G., ed. The Trend of Economics. New York, 1924.

Tugwell, Rexford G. Industry's Coming of Age. New York, 1927.

_____. The Industrial Discipline and the Governmental Arts. New York, 1933.

_____. "The Price Also Rises," Fortune, v. 9, January 1934, 70-72, 107-108.

Twentieth Century Fund. Financing American Prosperity: A Symposium of Economists. New York, 1945.

United States Government. Report of the Committee on Recent Economic Change, Recent Economic Changes in the United States, 2 v. New York, N.B.E.R., 1929.

_____. Temporary National Economic Committee, Senate doc., 77th Cong., 1st Sess. Final Report of the Executive Secretary. Washington, 1941.

Veblen, Thorstein. The Theory of the Leisure Class. New York, 1912.

_____. The Engineers and the Price System. New York, 1921.

_____. Absentee Ownership and Business Enterprise in Recent Times: The Case of America. New York, 1923.

Villard, Henry H. "Some Aspects of the Capacity to Produce," American Economic and Statistical Review, v. 21, February 1939, 15-18.

Williams, John H. "Deficit Spending," American Economic Review, Proceedings, v. 30, February 1941, 52-66.

Wilson, Thomas. Fluctuations in Income and Employment. London, 1942.

Wright, David McCord. "The Great Guessing Game," Review of Economic Statistics, v. 28, February 1946, 18-22.

Secondary Materials

American Economic Association. Readings in Business Cycles, v. 10. Homewood, Ill., 1965.

Barger, Harold. The Management of Money. Chicago, 1964.

Bining, Arthur C., and Thomas Cochran. The Rise of American Economic Life. New York, 1964.

Domar, Evsey. "Expansion and Employment," American Economic Review, v. 27, March 1947, 34-55.

Dorfman, Joseph. The Economic Mind in American Civilization, v. 5. New York, 1959.

_____. "The Background of Institutional Economics," in Institutional Economics. Berkeley, 1964, 1-44.

Duesenberry, James S. Income, Saving, and the Theory of Consumer Behavior. Cambridge, Mass., 1949.

_____. Business Cycles and Economic Growth. New York, 1958.

Eckhaus, R. "The Accelerator Principle Reconsidered," Quarterly Journal of Economics, v. 67, May 1963, 209-230.

Fellner, William. Trends and Cycles in American Economic Activity. New York, 1956.

Fox, Daniel M. The Discovery of Abundance: Simon N. Patten and the Transformation of Social Theory. Ithaca, 1967.

Freidel, Frank. Franklin D. Roosevelt: The Triumph. Boston, 1956.

Friedman, Milton, and Anna J. Schwartz. A Monetary History of the United States, 1867-1960. Princeton, 1963.

Galbraith, John Kenneth. The Great Crash, 1929. Boston, 1954.

_____. The Affluent Society. Boston, 1958.

Gerschenkron, Alexander. Economic Backwardness in Historical Perspective: A Book of Essays. Cambridge, Mass., 1962.

Gordon, Robert A. "Cyclical Experience in the Interwar Period: The Investment Boom of the 1920's," in Conference on Business Cycles. New York, N.B.E.R., 1951, 163-215.

_____. Business Fluctuations. rev. ed. New York, 1961.

_____. "Institutional Elements in Contemporary Economics," in Institutional Economics. Berkeley, 1963, 123-147.

Gruchy, Allan G. Modern Economic Thought: The American Contribution. New York, 1947.

Haberler, Gottfried. _Prosperity and Depression,_ revised and expanded. Cambridge, Mass., 1958. Original ed., 1937.

Hansen, Alvin H. _A Guide to Keynes_. New York, 1953.

_____. _Business Cycles and National Income_. Expanded edition. New York, 1964.

Hansen, Alvin H. and Richard V. Clemence, eds. _Readings in Business Cycles and National Income_. New York, 1953.

Harris, Seymour E., ed. _Schumpeter: Social Scientist_. Cambridge, Mass., 1951.

_____. _American Economic History_. New York, 1961.

_____. _The New Economics: Keynes' Influence on Theory and Public Policy_. New York, 1965.

Hawley, Ellis W. _The New Deal and the Problem of Monopoly: A Study in Economic Ambivalence_. Princeton, 1966.

Hicks, John D. _Republican Ascendancy, 1921-1933_. New York, 1960.

Hicks, John R. _A Contribution to the Theory of the Trade Cycle_. Oxford, rev. ed., 1961.

Kalecki, M. _Theory of Economic Dynamics_. London, 1954, rev. ed., 1965.

Kirkland, Edward C. _A History of American Economic Life_. New York, 1951.

Klein, Lawrence R. _The Keynesian Revolution_. New York, 1949.

_____. _The Keynesian Revolution,_ expanded ed. New York, 1966.

Kravis, Irving B. "Relative Income Shares in Fact and Theory," _American Economic Review,_ v. 49, December 1959, 917-949.

Kuznets, Simon. _National Income, A Summary of Findings_. New York, N.B.E.R., 1946.

_____. _Capital in the American Economy, its Formation and Financing_. Princeton, N.B.E.R., 1961.

_____. "The Contribution of Wesley C. Mitchell," in _Institutional Economics_. Berkeley, 1963, 95-122.

Leuchtenburg, William E. _The Perils of Prosperity, 1914-1932_. Chicago, 1958.

Lewis, W. Arthur. _Economic Survey, 1919-1939_. London, 1949.

Matthews, R. C. O. _The Business Cycle_. Chicago, 1959.

May, Henry F. "Shifting Perspectives on the 1920's," _Mississippi Valley Historical Review_, v. 43, December 1956, 405-427.

Merlin, Sidney D. _The Theory of Fluctuations in Contemporary Economic Thought_. New York, 1949.

Meyer, John R., and R. R. Glauber. _Investment Decisions, Economic Forecasting, and Public Policy_. Boston, 1964.

Meyer, John R., and Edwin Kuh. _The Investment Decision: An Empirical Study_. rev. ed., Cambridge, Mass., 1966.

Mitchell, Broadus. _Depression Decade: From New Era Through New Deal, 1929-1941_. New York, 1947.

Mitchell, Wesley C., and Arthur F. Burns. _Measuring Business Cycles_. New York, N.B.E.R., 1946.

North, Douglass C. _Growth and Welfare in the American Past_. Englewood Cliffs, 1966.

Patterson, Robert T. _The Great Boom and Panic_. Chicago, 1965.

Prothro, James Warren. _The Dollar Decade_. Baton Rouge, 1954.

Roll, Eric. _A History of Economic Thought_. Englewood Cliffs, 1961, rev. ed.

Rostow, Walt W. _The Stages of Economic Growth: A Non-Communist Manifesto_. London, 1960.

Schlesinger, Arthur M. Jr. _The Age of Roosevelt_. 3 v. Cambridge, Mass., 1957 ff.

Schumpeter, Joseph A. _A History of Economic Analysis_. New York, 1954.

_____. _Capitalism, Socialism, and Democracy_, expanded ed. New York, 1950. Original ed., 1942.

Slichter, Sumner H. _What's Ahead for American Business_? Boston, 1951.

_____. _Economic Growth in the United States, Its History, Problems, and Prospects_. Baton Rouge, 1961.

Soule, George. _Prosperity Decade: From War to Depression, 1917-1929_. New York, 1947.

Universities-National Bureau Committee for Economic Research. _Conference on Business Cycles_. New York, N.B.E.R., 1951.

Williamson, Henry F. _Growth of the American Economy_. Englewood Cliffs, 1951.

Wright, Chester Whitney. _Economic History of the United States_. New York, 1949.

Index